Memoirs
Of
PFN

PAUL FERNAND NEDELEC

Copyright © 2018 Paul F Nedelec

All rights reserved.

ISBN-13:
978-1986569743

ISBN-10:
1986569748

DEDICATION

To my beautiful wife, my bride for life
and to my family, extended and all..

CONTENTS

Table of Contents

DEDICATION iii

ACKNOWLEDGMENTS i

FOREWORD 3

WHERE IT ALL BEGAN 5

    Mum 6

    Thomas Marie Nedelec 7

    The courtship? 8

    The Family 9

MEMORIES OF PRESCHOOL 10

    The Good Times 10

    The Bad 12

    The Highs 16

    The Lows 17

ELEMENTARY SCHOOL – VYNER 19

    The Good Times 19

    The Bad Times 20

    The Highs 21

HIGH SCHOOL, VAWN 23

  The Good times 23

  The Bad Times 26

  The Highs 32

ST. THOMAS COLLEGE 33

  The Good Times 33

  The Bad Times 33

WORK ON THE FARM 38

THE FIRST YEARS AWAY 40

  Staying with Louis and Lorraine 40

  Staying with Uncle Henry and Aunt Désirée 41

  Staying with Cousin Yvonne and Jacque Jenvrin 42

  Staying with The Beyers 43

COLD LAKE AIR BASE 44

BACK TO EDMONTON, 1955 47

URANIUM CITY 50

EDMONTON 54

CALGARY 57

EPILOGUE 67

ABOUT THE AUTHOR 68

HE LEFT FOOTPRINTS ON OUR HEARTS 71

ACKNOWLEDGMENTS

To my parents Delphine and Thomas,
To all my sibling especially for all the good times,
and to my mitsy peashell with all of her titles;
Chief Ghost Writer, Editor and Publisher and
WhatEverItTakesToGetTheJobDone

FOREWORD

By Michelle Nedelec

My father's name is Paul Fernand Nedelec, or as my mother used to always say it Paul F. Nedelec; PFN for short. Because of that I used to call him PFN Stuff, like dragon H.R. Pufnstuf. And, like a good happy dragon, my father seemed to me in a way to be imaginary; a character of literature. He was always the hero. He was always fun, even when he was seriously puttering around doing something very serious, it always seemed intriguing to me.

As you'll find out, if you don't already know, my father grew up in Saskatchewan with 9 siblings in his family, and he was number 8 out of 10. I, like my father, had numerous elder siblings, and by the time I came of age to play my elder siblings, they had moved out of the house. Like my father there wasn't a lot of storytelling, in my case just homework. But, when my siblings would return home, we had visitors, or even better yet we went back to visit his siblings the stories would fly from the table like medieval dragons and the magic would stir.

My cousin's used to tell me that they loved Uncle Paul because he always told great stories. And, he did. We'd all be listening with abated breath, in disbelief wondering what would happen next, or just wondering how they lived to tell the tales.

My father comes from another land and from another time. Without putting pen to paper, or voice to video, these stories might all be forgotten. I'm delighted that he decided to share those stories with me, so that I can share them with you. And, maybe together, we can keep the dragon's tales alive in our imaginations.

WHERE IT ALL BEGAN

I was born April 19, 1933! It seems like 100 years ago! Actually it's almost 85 to the day of this writing. I was born in a pig-barn. Or so the story goes. I was actually born at home. I think Mrs. McCaffery might have been there to help my mother. The reason my siblings used to tease me about being born in the pig-barn was because they were building a pig-barn at the time. I didn't talk much but before my siblings would tell anyone that I was born in a pig-barn, I would say it until my mother told me it wasn't very complimentary to her.

I was born the 8th of what would be 10 children to Thomas Marie Nedelec and Delphine (nee Blaquiere) who, I think, were married in 1919. I hope so anyway, because Roger was born in 1920. Before they were married he used to go out ice fishing on Turtle Lake. For shelter he would flip over the horse sleigh and sleep in hay, cow and buffalo hides. The hides were stiff but they could use the hay to tuck in around themselves. (We had a buffalo hide even when we were going to school; in the cutter. It sure was warm but it was stiff and you couldn't wrap yourself up in it.) They would commercial fish out of Jack Fish Lake. They took the fish to the rail road station in Vawn and they were shipped to restaurants in New York and Chicago. It was winter time so they were kept frozen the whole time.

I guess I should give you a little bit of history to my family, maybe it'll make it all make sense or maybe it's just a bit of a history lesson.

Mum

Born in January 10, 1894 to a family with one sister and three brothers in the beautiful part of southern France with the mild climate manicured forest and many vineyards that produced wonderful wine that made that part of the country famous. Mum did not work in the vineyard as a young girl but did work in the caves where the large rolls of Roquefort Cheese was stored, because of the temperature and humidity being just right for the aging process.

Her work involved rolling these large bulks at regular intervals to improve the curing more evenly.

Mum and her sister had to sell the land and buildings before leaving the home place as the brothers were all in Canada. That had been quite a responsibility for two young ladies and they felt that they had been taken advantage of. Women did not handle money or business deals in those days.

In all those years on the farm most women had very little say about running the show or spending money. Mum had a hard time getting money for clothing, shoes etc, for herself or the family. There were always funds available for a jug of wine, cigars and pip tobacco though. Strange eh?

Thomas Marie Nedelec

Born in Casque-sur-Casque in Brittainy France on the 5th of April 1886 to a fisherman father and a home keeping mother. Dad had one brother and two sisters and one half-sister. He migrated to Canada with his father and brother Corentin in 1903 and settled in St. Norbert Manitoba where grandpa was taking up a homestead. In 1904 grandpa had a tragic accident with an oxen and a horse hitched together on a hay-wrack. Somehow he had a hard time getting them going but when they did it was sudden which caused grandpa to fall off the load to the front and consequently run over.

The two young brothers moved to Vawn Saskatchewan in 1905 and took on their own homesteads. Uncle Corentin soon sold his quarter section to Dad and then took up a homestead in the Paradise Hill area.

It was a hard life having to clear ten acres a year to qualify for homesteader status. There were many trees to cut, roots to dig out and rocks to pick. After being a milk-man in the streets of Paris, I don't imagine he was in the best physical condition. His father had moved the family and all, and he worked as a blacksmith.

The courtship?

All these young lonely settlers would see each other once in a while, usually at church, and tell about their lovely sisters back home in the old country. Soon they would tell these same poor girls about the good-looking hard-working ambitious future farmers who desperately needed a wife and family. Because of the turmoil at the time with the first world war raging on, these lovelies were glad to correspond by slow mail and plan for their futures in the promised land.

My mother, being a sister to three local homesteaders was most likely contacted by all three and convinced into getting to know dad. She and her sister (Mrs. Guiho) sailed to Canada in 1919 after the 1st World War and the wedding bells were soon ringing. Roger was born in March 1920 and many more in short order.

Mum was from St. Affrique area in the Province district of southern France. Their soft-spoken dialect was much more refined than the harsh French spoken in Brittany. Needless to say the guys were quite established and set in their ways and routines and the young brides had to fit in and be quite submissive to their (quite often) domineering husbands.

The Family

The family history is vast, and we believe, quite interesting, but family tree alone is a book unto itself. We've listed the siblings and their spouses here as they get mentioned without reference later in the book.

1920, March 26 Roger; married Mildred
1921, September 3 George; married Josephine
1922, August 14 René; married Ann
1924, November 11 Lucien; married Louise
   Their son Robert took over the homestead.
   (Later mentioned as Robert)
1926, Nov 7 Marcel Died 1926
1928, June 6 Johnny; married Jenny
1930, April 2 Yvette; married George
1931, August 8 Andrew; married Mildred
1933, April 19 Paul; married Mary-Adele
1936, April 10 Charlie; married Jennifer
1939, April 30 Helen; married Jim

MEMORIES OF PRESCHOOL

The Good Times

Many fun times were had out in the open usually with Andrew and sometimes Johnny, and later with Charlie. Andrew and I spent many hours in the fields, bushes, sloughs and ditches. Springtime was exciting as we would watch the skies for the first ducks, geese, swans, robins, hawks, crows, cranes, woodpeckers and a multitude of small birds. Later in the spring a favourite pastime would be to watch many of these birds and trace their flights to their nests and eggs.

This skill and patience paid off later as we found many crow and magpie nests to collect a penny for each egg, paid by the municipality through the school. Andrew did most of the tree climbing and got to be real brave and good at it, whether it was going up a tall branchless poplar or spindly shaft Willows. Many falls were experienced over those early years but very few were reported.

We also made money from gopher tails. Gophers were usually caught by hauling many buckets of water from sloughs or ditches sometimes many yards from the gopher holes. Binder twine was the most common item used as there was normally a straw stack within sight. A time or two when water was not readily available or we didn't have a bucket (in school years our lunch lard buckets) with us being really ingenious we would stuff the gopher hole with dried prairie wool grass and set it on fire. After setting quite a large prairie fire ablaze with the help of a run-away gopher with its fur and grass on fire we had to give up that method.

We ran like crazy trying to stomp it out, but it didn't work. Finally we had to give up. Luckily there were alkali sloughs around it and it burnt out.

~~~

Many enjoyable hours were spent sneaking very slowly to be within viewing distance to watch the spring mating dances of the prairie chicken, actually sharp tail grouse, and a few lucky instances of the Sandhill crane. It was quite interesting. The Sharp tail grouse, for the mating season would have their head down low, their wings spread out, and would be jumping around to impress the females. But, with the Sandhill cranes, they would spread their wings, but they would jump high, jumping up and down, and making their peculiar noise at the same time.

~~~

Many times we nailed and tied together with old binder twine old boards or poles to form a makeshift Huck Finn raft to explore the great treasures of our spring sloughs. The most interesting waterhole was the willow circled one about a mile southwest of home.

The pig pen or yard which is now the lawn northeast of Lucien and Louise's house did flood a few springs. Rather than walk and carry logs or boards to a distant slough, Andrew and I decided to use a metal water trough for a makeshift boat or canoe. I think Charlie was even involved in a few of these episodes. Needless to say there was nothing very stable about this craft and we ended up mighty wet and much stinkier than from our regular slough water. Our mother put up with having to do some mighty stinky laundry.

At that time Andrew might have been 10 years old, so I would have been about 8 ½ and Charlie would be 5 ½. Can you imagine a poor little 5 ½ year old coming home after swimming through the pig's slough?

Andrew didn't start school until he was 7 because his birthday was in August, or possibly because he didn't want to go. I guess we played in the sloughs for quite a few years.

This was definitely preschool;

One thing Andrew and I enjoyed was playing in the piles of dirty laundry while Mum was doing the washing. The noise and vibration of the washing machine's gas engine often put us to sleep which my mother didn't mind. Peace at Last! I'm quite convinced now that the fumes are what put us under.

There were quite a bit of fumes. I'm not sure how mum put up with it. When you go in the house from the west side, eventually there was a washroom built there, but at that time, it was open and the washing machine was there.

The Bad

The bad part of my preschool years would have to be that Andrew and I did not spend much time with our older siblings or parents. We hardly ever saw our neighbors or relatives and when they did come to visit we knew that we had to stay out of sight. How did they expect us to learn!? We were expected to speak French at home but we were learning a few English words from the older siblings so, Andrew and I, our language became a mixture of French, English and baby talk.

It was sad. I think Andrew was a little worse than I was because he was older, he was expected to speak better than he did. But even his name, André, in French instead of calling himself that or Aré, he would call himself Ké. If he wanted something he would say, "Ké, veux."

Even at an older age, to the extent that it used to bug me and I would correct him. He had a hell of a time adjusting especially in school it was tough.

~~~

We spent hardly any time at all with the older kids, even Johnny being five years older than me; we hardly spent any time at all with him. When he came home he had chores to do. Although sometimes, we did managed to hang around them when they were milking the cows.

Little wonder we became really shy and refuse to associate with others when the occasion arose as they had great difficulty understanding us. I remember well the time that Uncle Henry told Mom and Dad that we were either mighty shy or stupid because we didn't answer when spoken to. It really hurt because he was one of my favourite uncles. I don't know why but maybe it was because he took a little time to get to know us.

This problem (shy or stupid) made going to school and learning anything including socializing real difficult. We slowly adopted as we discovered that others (some) we're in the same boat. Not quite.

The Plourds were French, but they didn't speak French at school. The McNutts, I think the mother was native. The father and older brother were in the army. Melvin was quite lively and had a really nice horse. They didn't have much money but for some reason he had a really nice horse named Zip. It was a nice riding horse. Then there was Bernice, Vera and Muriette, I think it was; there were three girls. And, eventually Clarence; he was the baby. But, they were real poor. There were only about four or five families. Eventually the Nahirney's moved in. They were real shy. They spoke Ukrainian at home. Oksanna was a cute little girl and there were three more after her; Michael and Peter, and William. Being Ukrainian they were expected to study and work hard. They did work hard and did well later on in school. William, Charlie used to associate with him. He moved to Kelowna and ran a helicopter business and did real well. The other two stayed on the farm and did quite well. But the oldest one, I think was putting up the money and they put up a seed cleaning plant close to North Battleford. Apparently they were doing well but then because of William's ambition, he wanted them to expand and expand, so they did. They did to the extent that Peter was working long hours, and I don't know if he was overly exhausted or fed up with the whole works, but he ended up committing suicide. It ended up hitting the district really hard.

~~~

Being one of the younger of the siblings meant less contact with Mom or Dad and more with our older brothers in the evenings. That, I think, has created a close-knit unit except for Rodger who left home at an early age and did not stay in close contact after coming home from France in '47 and going to Victoria.

I felt that we were not encouraged to do well in school or try to exceed in anything except work. Success meant possible pride and false pride was a sin.

It was sad. My mum didn't talk much but my father had his opinions. It was so bad that if Yvette or Johnny, it was usually Yvette, or Johnny to some extent but not much, certainly not Andrew or I, would say something he would make it known that if you were proud of any accomplishment that it was a sin.

Yvette, later on when she was in high school or earlier, she used to read quite a bit and would talk to dad about what they had been reading. That's something that Johnny and Lucien, and Rène I'm sure would not do. Andrew and I we never did. We weren't encouraged to read and we didn't have much of anything there to read anyway. We never got any newspapers or anything. Mum didn't have time to read, she might have in the afternoon when everyone was gone. She certainly didn't discuss anything she had read, anyway. And, when George and Rène came back from overseas in '45, they went to Trail BC. They worked there and stayed with Bob and Vi Rogers, Ann's parents. (Vi was her step mother) They stayed there for a couple of years but then George got his VLA land (Vetran's Land Act land) so he came back to Saskatchewan. But at lunch time and meal time the only discussion was dad and George talking politics or religion. Lucien would never say anything. Johnny, Yvette, Andrew and I wouldn't say anything. Mum didn't say anything. She was busy serving. George was the only one that worked up the gumption to disagree with Dad.

When he first came back he found out that our school teacher was quite a nice young lady so he dated her a time or two. But this one night, he forgot to come home. When he did come home at breakfast time Dad was giving him hell right at the breakfast table which I figured was terribly out of place and I almost felt like laughing. I didn't dare.

Dad was quite negative and he figured whatever had happened, it had to have been sinful. It had to be bad. He didn't give George the opportunity to explain that it had been tough being in the war and that it had been devastating. I'm sure that he suffered from Post-Traumatic Stress Disorder, but nobody knew what that was and nobody bothered asking. It was so bad that George said at one point that at night he would hear noises in the stairs and he'd have to check and see that it wasn't the Germans coming up the stairs. Needless to say, he didn't sleep well. But, he did stay home until he married Josie.

Lucien cooperated with him as far as helping him get set up. There wasn't any financial arrangement. It was the same as when I spent lots of my spare time after school, on weekends and stuff, helping George with no money and no agreement. When I finally asked he said, "Well you're getting free room and board aren't you?"

My answer had to be, "Well, you're not paying for it!"

He was getting free room and board as well!

The main reason I figured that George had some damage done to him was the fact that he adopted Rose which, unfortunately, was a very big mistake. He never did like natives. He figured they were third class citizens. When I asked him why he adopted, he said, "Well I'm paying school taxes. I might as well benefit from it."

A real loving attitude, eh?

However, when I was at St. Tomas College he was the only one of the bunch that ever stopped in to see me. I never heard from Dad or Mom or Yvette or Lucien. It was quite a lowly rough time.

The Highs

The highs of my preschool years had to be the time that was spent with family.

Mom was always there busy and often over tired but always very kind and loving to everyone. She was a terrific cook, housekeeper, launderer, mender, and alterer of clothing, sheets, curtains Etc. Clothing as well as many other items were recycled many times. There was a hell of a lot of work to do there.

We had some outside games including many siblings but nothing indoors.

I recall Dad being real good walking around on stilts that George had made; a rare occasion. He was fairly athletic apparently when he was younger. He was a good swimmer, apparently, although none of us were. He walked on the stilts like there was nothing to it, and the feet on them were about three feet high. I don't think I ever saw him ride the bicycle, but we just had one sort of broken down bicycle.

The Lows

The lows during my preschool years were when the older brothers were leaving home to work for neighbors and eventually leaving to work in Niagara Falls and then World War II.

My loneliest year had to be when Andrew took off to Vyner for grade one. He was seven in August and I would have been five and a half and Charlie three and a half. Charlie was not the outdoors type so then I was the one lost soul. I tagged along behind dad as Lucien, the only other one home during the day, was busy. That did not pay off in the least. No bonding to be had.

I tried to bond with Dad, but he didn't have any time or use for me. One time I wanted his attention, we were out in the yard and the neighbour, Phillip McCaffery, was there. Eddie's father. Phillip and Dad were talking and I kept saying, "Dad! Dad! Dad!"

And, he'd ignore me. So finally, you can figure out that at five and a half years old I wanted his attention, so I pushed him from behind. He wasn't expecting me to do that, so he sort of stumbled. He turned around and with one great big clout he hit me.

After that I never did go close to him again.   Never.

I had tried to forget about it, but 10 maybe 20 years ago, I asked John why I was never close to Dad. He was amazed that I had forgotten. I asked what happened. He told me. And, all of a sudden it came back. I was quite bitter. It hurt. What's worse is that it was at quite the early stage when I realized that this was the end of it.

I asked Charlie time before last when we saw him, if he was close to Dad, and he wouldn't even answer.

When we were in England, trying to get to know Roger (~1990's). I asked him about Dad and he was quite proud of him, but you can imagine being the first born son, Dad being so much younger and everything went well. Roger was born in '21, he worked for Webbers and different neighbours before the war around '43, so he might have been 20 or so when he left. He had some good years with Dad, so he was quite amazed that I never had any relationship with him.

Both George and Roger went to Niagara Falls before the war. They got along with each other and Dad. Rene could get along with anybody. And, Lucien was so easy going. He did his work and he did his best. Sometimes with Dad's advice but Lucien took over at a young age. I don't think he even got grade eight. He had to work on the farm. The army didn't conscript him because of his age; he was still too young at the time. But when the time did come they accepted that he was needed on the farm. He learned from experience, and he took a course or two. I think it was a welding course in North Battleford and that helped him. He never took a mechanical course but he did well!

ELEMENTARY SCHOOL – VYNER

The Good Times

The real challenge was to learn to speak proper English and to learn how to get along with kids from grades one to grade eight. The Fondest Memories have to be the runs in the woods with the older students who will be hunting with slingshots for bush rabbits or wood partridges. We grade ones and twos were told to circle around the patches of badger-brush willows or at times thistles and then close in to bring in the game.

~~~

The lonely, isolated, rough life imposed on our usually young, inexperienced teachers meant yearly change of teachers. Some were dedicated while others were quite a pain.

~~~

A pleasant experience was bringing to school our cache of crow and magpie eggs, and gopher tails for the big buyout. We might have caught fifty each. We used to go to North Battleford once a year. (52Km) We were happy to spend five cents for a chocolate bar or, I think it was fifty cents for an ice cream sundae. That was a lot of money then! Yvette and Johnny didn't bother. By the time Charlie came along the municipality didn't pay anymore.

It was the same for Johnny, as those before. He didn't finish grade eight, and he worked for different neighbours. He made a little bit of money and that's when he started going to dances. He worked for Stockford, a farmer that was north of Vawn on the west side of the road and then, the Bellans which was just across the road half a mile or so. Both Johnny and Rene worked a time for Uncle Marius but they didn't have very good reports on him. He was a miserable one!

The Bad Times

The worst problem was having TB...tiny bladder...and, having to go to the Outhouse too often for the teachers liking. Often the teacher would ignore this shy kid with his hand up waving desperately to the extent that after seeing me no longer waiving at flies but no crying with my coveralls obviously wet. That and my bed wetting problem and poor bathing habits was not conducive to attracting any close friendships.

I don't know how the teachers ever put up with that. You can imagine going back to the school with my winter underwear and combination coveralls all wet! It made it pretty hard to concentrate, especially with the others staring at me, everyone from grade one through eight in one room.

~~~

Not knowing how to play with kids my age because we didn't have close neighbours, I often got into a beating from trying to pester older kids (usually girls) and testing their limits.

After a few times of having my face plastered with mud or snow or being choked by having two thumbs to the throat, I just had to smarten up. That meant staying to myself and going into a shell. Even the teachers over the years seem to appreciate that.

The Highs

As with many modern kids the recesses were the best part of school. Quite often the older students would organize a scrub game of ball when each player would move up one position to being at bat. The batter would stay at bat until struck out or got taken out at one of the bases. There were three batters at a time.

~~~

The other high had to be the few field trips organized by Miss Square or the small bush trips on our own. Being outdoors farm kids most of us really enjoyed the field trips to the hills at Turtle Creek. In the summer we'd take a ball and bat and play ball, or walk around in the bushes a bit. But, at least it was time away from school. I think John was still in school at that time, and we'd take a team of horses and a wagon. One time we went out in winter time with toboggans, sleds and an old set of skis with a makeshift strap. It didn't take much to make a change from being at school. Although we might not have done much, I sure enjoyed them

Some of the games were scrub ball game, anti-i over (over the school roof), prisoner's base or hide and seek. In the winter we had snow ball fights or making snowmen, or playing fox and the goose. That's when you have a circle in the snow, the person that was it would be the fox in the middle. The geese with sheer numbers try to box in the fox so that he cannot move. The fox, on the other hand, is trying to capture geese so it becomes impossible for them to trap him.

~~~

We tried building a skating rink around the pump but that never worked out as we didn't know how, and it was also too dangerous as it was half way between the school and the teacherage. No one had skates anyhow.

~~~

This one teacher, Clifford Thompson took a liking to her and he would come around. She gave us the impression that she wasn't interested. Quite often if he would drive by she would just get lost. So this one time we froze a piece of firewood into the ice with a rabbit snare over the path in hopes of catching him. Instead we caught the teacher! We got hell over that. She told us about it and apparently she had quite the tumble. So there was no more of that!

HIGH SCHOOL, VAWN

The Good times

New challenges and new friends. Many students we knew by name or at least had heard about their parents. Good thing for me my big sister, Yvette, had a couple years' experience with the big-times before me. She was the first in our family to go on to high school which was a real luxury at the time. Many of our older brothers would have benefited immensely had they been able to go on with their education.

~~~

Yvette walked to school but I used a bicycle in summer and horseback in winter.

In the cold of the winter we used the horses and caboose. I didn't miss my chances of letting my "pain in the neck" sister know what a troublesome chore it was to harness and unharness and feed and water the horses because of her. Later when Yvette went on to convent in North Battleford, I rode my white mare Dolly bareback summer and winter.

The few moments of pride in those years were when someone noticed that I was the only cowboy coming to school in that fashion. I often wondered since, if I smelled accordingly.

The way they got to school; the closer ones walked, some rode their bicycles. In the winter most got rides. The main road, the highway was open. Webbers were right on the highway. And, the road going north and south, I'm quite sure that road was kept open in the winter too. I'm sure they got rides and some of them even walked quite the distance.

The way I got my horse Dolly was quite sad. She was a real nice horse and a good horse. But this one time, years before, Dad was fixing something on the machinery and Dolly didn't know he was there or maybe a fly bothered her or whatever, she took a kick in the air. She didn't hit him but he got mad and hit her with the hammer that he had. He could have hit her on the cheeks of her rear end, but he hit her right in the backbone to the extent that it crippled her up. She could never pull a load again after that. She always pulled sideways. She wasn't any good to anybody not even on the buggy or the cutter. I was the only one then that was riding anywhere, so I was able to claim her as my horse.

It was strange. Even as she was trotting she was going sideways because of the pain but if I let her gallop she would straighten up. She liked to gallop. In winter time my hands would get cold trying to hold her back, so I would drop the reigns and put my hands under my armpits to keep them warm. We'd do that all the way to Vawn and it was the same thing coming home.

The same Marlene Webber that I was talking about earlier, I was quite proud when she insisted that I let her take my picture on the horse. I never did get a copy of it.

~~~

We did have some organized ball games in the summer and I did play a few games but never in competition with other schools. Being an overgrown farmer with two left feet, I was reminded time and again that I had to make a home run hit just to get to first base.

~~~

In the winter the hockey rink, close to the school, was the all-important place to be. The one and only sport indoor was our tennis table. The girls didn't show much interest in this so we guys had the control of times allotted to different players. Bill Brownridge, my seatmate over three years, and Pete Vermette who sat behind us were the top players. I came a distant third after much practice and some pretty intense competition.

~~~

Learning and remembering anything was a real chore but I knew that high school education was a must if I was to leave the farm. Little did I realize that it would be even for those wanting to take up farming for a living too. At that time they were starting to realize that farmers needed to be educated too.

By that time, there were different ones like Bert and Johnny Blaquiere went to college in Edmonton. They were doing well and getting ahead. There were a few from St. Hippolyte, Vawn, and Edam that went to Gravelbourg and seemed to be happy and looking forward to the future. So I figured I should do the same thing. The main thing about going to St. Thomas College is that I knew if I tried to get grade 12 at home, I still wouldn't be doing homework, I'd be trying to make money selling firewood and there was no hope in that.

The Bad Times

The hard time throughout high school was the fact that I, along with many other problems, had not learned how to read properly and did not absorb what I read in many cases. Being too shy or maybe proud I didn't question when I didn't understand something and quite often did not complete assignments. Not once except exam time maybe, do I remember doing homework or review. Mom and Dad certainly didn't ask if I had done my homework. If there were checkups done then I'm sure I would have been diagnosed with Attention Deficit Syndrome. Many a time I would be sitting, while the teacher was talking, thinking that I should be somewhere else doing something different.

~~~

Two winters in a row I hauled a sleigh load of firewood to Vawn on school days to sell in town after school. This entailed chopping and loading the wood after supper, then in the morning feeding, harnessing, hitching, and then unhitching at Louis Vallieres livery barn then walk about half a mile to the school. Then after school hitching up and peddling that load of wood and then the slow ride home. It took quite a bit longer compared to horseback galloping all the way home. This was the ritual for a load that sold for $5 to me and $5 to George. I figured making big money was more important than going to school.

I figured out then, though, that if I wanted to get half decent marks in grade 12 that I needed to get out of Vawn because I wasn't getting any homework done. I wasn't getting ahead that way! In fact I failed two subjects in grade 11.

The Lows in high school were basically the same as in grade school. My bed-wetting problem was not as severe as in the earlier years, but there were times I'm sure when I should have had a bath after a bad night but that was unheard of with chores to do and a long haul to school. With the long haul too, I'm sure I stunk of sweat and horses too.

~~~

Besides this for a worry, there was also the problem of a few times of falling asleep in school at the most awkward times. A real low was being sent to the only other room to learn grade 8 French for the first time. When asked to conjugate a verb I was dumbfounded and just sat there. The teacher thought I was being stubborn and threw her book at me.

Because of the name Nedelec, they thought I should be quite fluent in French.

Without speaking a word of either French or English I got up and sauntered back to my regular seat in grade 9 in the high school room.

~~~

The McCafferys were good friends of Mom and Dad's and the kids were many and the same ages as our family. During the war years when the three older siblings were away we would spend Christmas day there and they would come over for New Year's or vice versa. We had great times for sure. They worked hard and farmed well and prospered. We weren't quite so ambitious and lagged behind terribly.

They went into purebred cattle and that paid off. I think they had much better soil than we did. We had really sandy soil. Also, Dad wouldn't let us work on Sundays which cost us money. With others, if they had to harvest, they did!

This one year especially we had to depend on Webbers or LaCashiers to thrash our crop, but we were the last on the list almost. Webbers called and said they were ready to move in and Dad said, "Well, we don't harvest on Sundays."

So, they said, "OK," and moved on to the next neighbour. By the time they finished work with the next neighbour, it snowed, so our crops stayed outside. Then the mice got into it over the winter and we lost a lot of the crop. You can't get rich farming like that. There were different things that I didn't agree with but, Dad was the boss.

~~~

One thing that really bothered me is the fact that Dad's sister, Jane Delisle, her husband had left her and she had the two sons, Harvey and Joe. They stayed with her, and then once they were old enough, they took off and went east.

We never once had her over for a meal. We hardly ever heard about her. We would pick her up only at Christmas midnight mass. That was the only time we would take her to mass. Other than that, Dad never even took any food over to her, or clothing or anything.

Dave St. Marie, living across the road farther north, he would spend some time with her and looked after her.

But, it was the same with Henry Forgue. You heard of George Forgue? Well George married Rose. (Rose being my brother George's adopted daughter) His father was Robert. He was one of the three sons. There was Robert, Joe and Phillip. They couldn't handle him at Vawn anymore so they sent them to Vyner. They were obviously poor. But, when I was going to school in Vawn I would see Henry's horse and buggy or cutter, at the beer parlor. The kids were abused terribly and there were a few times I mentioned it to Dad, the fact that Henry was drunk and whipping his horse all the way home, but Dad never did anything about it. He could preach the bible and go by the bible but there were a hell of a lot of times where he didn't practice what he preached.

I don't know what the problem was dealing with his sister Jane, whether he blamed her for her husband taking off on her, but there were definitely some hard felt feeling for some reason. And it says right in the bible, "Don't come to me unless first you have reconciled with your brother."

Another time was when they were building that hall in Vawn. They wanted stones for the footings, and we had a whole bunch of stones lined up along the fence that we had picked amongst the years. They asked for those stones, but Dad said, "No way. Don't touch them."

He didn't contribute or have any part in helping with the hall.

~~~

Meanwhile, the McCafferys became quite proud and arrogant and George, who was my age, quite often made it clear that I didn't belong in his circle of friends that is except if he wanted something.

I let this build up in me for years and then one day on the way home from school he was walking and me on my high horse I proceeded to tell him exactly what I thought of him and the whole family. Except for the Women, they were fine. George had to finally beller at me to tone it down as we were getting close to his home and his mother would be asking questions. I was embarrassed about this for years after although I think it helped in the long run.

~~~

Bullying is not a new invention. Two of my so called friends George McCaffery and Paul Dion used to have a great time embarrassing me as much as possible. When I first went to Vawn for grade 8 and 9 I knew George McCaffery to a certain extent through. They were both active in ball and hockey; they were in pretty good shape. But, I was an intruder. At recess time, I guess it was obvious that I was alone. They took to the practice of one of them would pretend to be real friendly while the second would crouch down behind me and the first would push me backwards over top of him. So I learned I had to avoid them. But, they kept doing it even if I was real careful. I knew I had to do something, but if I got one of them down, the other one would jump me.

I realized I had to get them both at the same time. So I waited and waited until I got my chance. When they were both standing together I jumped them and got an arm around each of their necks, one on each side to the extent that I could hold on. They were kicking and knocking their elbows in my ribs and stuff, so I would tighten up on their necks some more until they were begging for mercy. I said, "Only if you promise to leave me alone from now on."

They didn't want to promise me so I tightened up a bit more! By then they were spitting and sputtering. I was determined to put an end to it, so I squeezed even harder. Finally they both promised, and sure enough they left me alone.

But, two guys I knew a bit, and thought we could be friends, I had to ignore them and avoid them and my so called friends avoided me ever since.

I'm lucky I had Bill Brownridge all those years.

~~~

Lloyd Webber was Marlene's brother. He was quite a nice guy, but I didn't associate with him too much because he was German and at that point I wasn't too happy with the Germans. But, he's the guy that took sick and died that first year.

At that time with my twisted thinking, I was thinking, "What goes around comes around." Leonard was a big time operator and expanding. Earl and John, the younger brothers, were having some sort of squabble. Earl kicked John and ruptured his spleen or whatever it was and Earl died. John eventually became a drinker and a fighter. He married Therese Cadrin, a real nice woman and also from a rich family; quite a big family with lots of money. But, that ended up in divorce because of his drinking and fighting. And then Lloyd died in grad twelve. And then Bill took over the farm, he married a cousin to Louise Nedelec (Lucien's wife). And he died at an early age. Leonard, the rich guy, died in his 60's. Kay Webber married a guy from North Battleford, I think he was a photographer. She died at an early age.

However, "Judge not, lest you be judged."

The Highs

The Highs of my high school years had to be meeting new people and also broadening my scope or outlook on life and seeing that there were many opportunities in life even for we poor forty acre farmers. Paul Julien was from the rich Julien family north of St. Hippolyte. He was there too in school taking grade 12. When we had our sports day to compete to see who qualified to play against other schools, he could throw the ball a long distance and he could do everything well and I couldn't. For that, he called me a forty acre farmer. That's the worst insult he could think of at the time. Somehow if you could only afford a forty acre farm, then you were no good at sports either.

~~~

Miss Oleo Arsenault was a brilliant and dedicated teacher for grades 9-11 but naturally spent most of her time helping those that showed the most promise and interest.

~~~

The best thing for sure was that Bill Brownridge was my seat mate and main opponent in Ping-Pong. The last time I saw Bill I asked him why he remained by bench mate for grades 9 to 11 and I think it was because we were sitting right next to the tennis table. We would race to get the bats and balls first. But it was also because of his crippled leg that he felt a bit lesser than the others. He was smart in school, but did have some feelings of being unworthy because of being crippled up. So that's why we stuck together.

ST. THOMAS COLLEGE

The Good Times

Everything was new with many new faces, ideas and rules. The meals were fair and the classrooms clean. The teachers who were German Oblate priests were on the whole smart and dedicated. There was a well-organized team and league in baseball in summer and hockey in winter but nothing for the amateurs. For the amateurs the college had compulsory Army Cadets which to me was not a sport. And, yes that was the extent of the good times.

The Bad Times

Most of the students there were of German decent from rich German families. Because of the fact that we had been fighting the Germans, and the only Germans we knew back home pretty well were the Webbers, they were a nice family and they did well. In fact, Marlene was one grade behind me in Vawn and she was a real nice girl. But the thing I didn't like was the fact that she had a whole bunch of brothers and they were not conscripted in the army because they were of German decent. But, in the meantime, different farmers were losing their sons to the war. They couldn't expand and in some cases needed to give up. This, allowed the Germans to buy land real cheap and to expand. Leonard Webber was the richest person in the district.

So going to school, I was quite bitter about that. And, having most of the kids in the school being the rich Germans, because they had the same opportunities, and most of the priests were German.

I didn't want any part of anything dealing with the military or any reference to war especially if it was promoted by the so called (Germans). With this attitude and my heavy schedule I resented any such thing being compulsory. The priest in charge oddly enough was the only non-German of the clan and seemed to think he had something to prove.

Some of the sergeants were grade 10 or 11 and had been doing this since day one so were highly qualified to be barking orders to this clumsy two left foot stumbling around on the parade square. Often I would be preoccupied wondering who had won the war or contemplating poking them right in the snout.

~~~

Two war veterans had come to St. Thomas College to complete their grade 12. Nice guys except for the fact that they took great pleasure in showing us young rookies gruesome postcards of corpses in open graves etc. and inside of concentration camps.

~~~

The school year did not begin on time due to the fact that the buildings were not ready for occupancy. Even when they did open a month late it was too soon. Before getting into bed we had to be sure to shake off our sheets and blankets which were covered in dust from the grinding down of the unfinished Torazo Tile floors.

~~~

On Friday afternoons we were sometimes allowed time off so I would go to a movie theater about 6 blocks away, which was fun. The problem was that we were expected to be back in time for prayers before the movies were finished. I had quite a time convincing our Prefect of Discipline, Farther Riffle, that I couldn't afford to waste my small amount of money on half a movie, and that taking in a movie once in a while was my only break in a heavy routine. No more extra prayers in the chapel after that.

~~~

Father Herman was a tall athletic type and quite a pleasant person but he felt quite free to slap me across the back of my head when most unexpected. It might have happened a time or two because I was drifting off, but I'm sure he must have regarded me has the bottom of the pecking order and not likely to retaliate in any way or report to any authority. That was another thing that sure buggered up my self-esteem.

~~~

My lows, or whatever one might call my condition at the time, were so bad that I wasn't sleeping well and on a couple occasions actually wet the bed. At that age and in a wide open dorm full of well bred, well raised young men, it was one more set back.

~~~

As if I needed anything else to knock me down my tonsils were getting mighty sore, but like so many years gone by the best way out was to grin and bear it until the swelling went down. Lo and behold that didn't help and sure enough to the emergency room in a hurry because one morning (apparently) I couldn't breathe. I don't remember any part of this.

Somebody reported it and got me to the hospital. The operation on swollen tonsils was long and bloody. When finally out of sedation my throat felt as if it had been cut off.

Doctor Breton, who had also been Mom's doctor, later informed me that I quit breathing and they had discovered a blood clot had broken loose and was going down my air passage. Can you imagine the tools or tricks trying to capture a soft gob way down my throat? After a week in the hospital I was back at STC and attending classes. I don't remember how I got to the hospital or back to STC but I do remember not seeing or hearing from anyone from home. They may have not even known what was happening.

~~~

My throat still hurt after I returned to classes to the point that I couldn't talk. I tried to concentrate and study, but it was mighty hard. Eventually, after a month or so, I tried to talk, but nobody could understand me. So then I gave up all together and I didn't talk to anybody for the last three months. Although there were 30 or so kids in the class, they must have given up on me too, because no one even tried to talk to me either. There was Roger Evesque from Paradise Hill, Ray Day from Cochen, and Denis Laboisier. They would say hi, but that was about it.

~~~

On top of all this I still had to redo the two subjects I had failed in grade 11. I think it was biology and geometry.

~~~

All in all, I was glad to get out of there. I don't even know what marks I got, but they told me I passed. I got a piece of paper saying I passed grade 12, but without any marks on it or anything. I was happy for that because then I could at least go looking for a job and tell them I got my grade 12.

At that time, it was quite a few years ago, if you were from the farm you had a good chance of getting a job. They knew you could drive. They knew you had some experience with some mechanical stuff.

WORK ON THE FARM

We were trained at an early age to be productive and to do our share. If we ever complained about being bored there was always wood to be split in winter or garden that needed hoeing or weeding in the summer and fall. We all learned to handle horses at a very young age. The apprentice stage was feeding, watering and lots of cleaning out the barn, chicken coop and pig pens. Usually it was Johnny and at times Lucien that was our trainer.

~~~

Cow milking came early as well but fetching them from the fields and bushes came sooner. Andrew and I took turns at this chore but there were times when it was raining and / or windy and it would be Andrew's turn to find the cows. John and Lucien would be ready to milk and there were no cows to be had and Andrew was nowhere to be found. Guess whose turn it suddenly became to get those blooming animals.

In such rain or wind conditions the cows would seek shelter in the thickest woods possible. They would be perfectly still which meant that their telltale bells would not be ringing at all. Quite often by this time it would be getting late and quite dark.

Onetime after all this Andrew still didn't show up for supper. Our aunt was staying with us for a while and she is the one that accidently found Andrew fast asleep under the sewing machine. I was ready to kill him by then.

~~~

Our farm was finally blessed with a mechanical horse shortly after the war. Uncle Henry had a garage and dealership in Edam and was able to convince Dad of the need for a fine little Ford Ferguson Tractor along with the three point hitch for the 2 furrow plow, cultivator and whatever equipment Lucien altered to fit this newfangled hydraulic lift. Dad was the only operator for quite some time while we were stuck to using the horses.

There was no incident of a runaway tractor but we had a few over the years with the horses. One case I remember was when Andrew was going into a field with two horses on the hay rake. Somehow he hit one of the gate posts with a wheel. His excuse was that the gateway was too narrow on one side.

~~~

Most of my faux-pas came much later in life. After leaving the farm for big city life I would always go back on my holidays. Everyone was busy at something so I was glad to join in and help. On one occasion we were camping at George and Yvette's (under the big tree directly south of the house) and George had me operate one of his tractors cultivating a field along with him on his outfit. After a short time he drove over and informed me that my tractor was smoking too much. I had forgotten to take it out of road gear. What a rookie.

~~~

Many years later I was helping my nephew, Robert, with cutting his hay crop. I was told to refuel after lunch so I did. In a short time I realized that I was putting gas in the hydraulic oil tank. I had never seen a piece of machinery with such a large hydraulic oil tank. It was a good thing that these farmers were tolerant and patient with green horns from the city. What a waste of time and fuel and oil. I should have been fired on the spot.

THE FIRST YEARS AWAY

Staying with Louis and Lorraine

They were good to me but they had not planned on having a boarder so they were quite relieved to have me move out. But, in the meantime Louis helped me to find my first car. It was the one that the kids used to play in at the backyard into the '70s. It was a burgundy 1953 Ford Mercury. The car was terrific and gave me all kinds of freedom that I haven't experienced before. I was able to go to work without having to ride the bus. That was even the car that I took Mary-Adele on our first date in. We went and saw The Hunchback of Notre Dame at the Uptown. She hid her eyes through half of it. But that was part of the plan, I would later say. But Mary-Adele says I wasn't fast enough; I was very polite. I thought I had fallen asleep, but that was another date. I had gone skiing with Mary-Adele, came home and went to the movies with another girl and was so tired I fell asleep. She was not very impressed. That was the end of that. However, the car made it through and I even taught Mary-Adele to drive in that car. But I didn't teach her how to back seat drive. She learned that on her own! The best part of the new car was the freedom and a chance with the girls! I can't blame the car for me falling asleep, though.

Although Louis was only 5 or 6 year other than me, Louis and Lorraine were full of confidence and ambition which gave me some incentive to do likewise.

Staying with Uncle Henry and Aunt Désirée

They were good to me and helpful in many ways. Uncle Henry got me a job with a friend of his at a service station to sell gas and wash vehicles. Despite being from the farm, I was quite nervous because I didn't have much experience with mechanical stuff. Sure enough, I goofed up when I was putting antifreeze in a vehicle. I knew that most of it would be water and a quarter of it was antifreeze. But, I put water in first, and I put too much in. There was so much so I couldn't put the whole bottle of antifreeze in. So that was wasted, and so was my job.

This was just before Christmas. I had no job and no money and Christmas came along. Aunty asked me to join them for Christmas dinner and I was too shy or too stupid. I said no, that I was going out, that I had been invited out. They knew darn well that it was a lie, but I think they were quite happy to get me out of the way. They had Helen Raboud and her family and Bob and Mary and their kids too. It was quite a houseful. I don't know if they had anybody else, but that's when I was walking the streets of Edmonton in the cold, dressed as if I was going to a party and not dressed to be walking the streets. But, I didn't dare go back to Uncle and Aunty's place because the party would still be on, so I stayed out there freezing.

Finally I figured I had better smarten up, "This is stupid. Stupid. Stupid." You gotta hit rock bottom before you change direction. I should have found a warm place to go, but I didn't. Eventually, long after dark, I went back and went to bed cold and hungry. I don't think I even had enough money to buy a meal.

~~~

Eventually, they had enough of me and referred me to Yvonne, one of the Nedelec's from St. Walburg, a sister to Louis, Marcel, Harvey, Albert, Anne, and Juliette.

Staying with Cousin Yvonne and Jacque Jenvrin

After uncle Henry booted me out I moved in with Yvonne and Jacque. The agreement was that I didn't have to pay rent but that I would babysit their kids every time they went out; which was quite often. The kids realized that I was nervous in the service. I had never really babysat before, other than Helen as a baby. They knew I was inexperienced and they made the most out of it.

~~~

Paul was handicapped at birth because his head was squeezed in delivery. He was about 10 at the time and the girls were all older. He was demanding attention and the girls would compete to throw me off guard. I was frustrated because I didn't know if their problems were real or not. I always had a tough time getting them to go to bed. They were supposed to do the dishes and clean up too, but they wouldn't. After they would finally go to bed, I would be the one who would get the chores done.

~~~

Jacque eventually got me a job with his good friend, Stan Sunley, and that's when I started in the electric trade.

Staying with The Beyers

Mrs. Beyers used to tease me about the girls because she knew how shy I was. At that time, I was dating a young lady. It was getting quite serious, but Mrs. Beyers would be teasing me about it and asking me questions. Mel Beyers could hardly hear because he had been working the crushing machine at the gravel pit. He was quite deaf.

This one time a girl left her bag in my vehicle. I checked and it was her underclothing, so I took it upstairs and laid it over my bed so that Mrs. Beyers would really have something to talk about.

She was harping on it and I was quite tired at supper time and Mrs. Beyers was yapping away. Finally, I was going to say, "You know, by the sound of things," I said, "it sounds as if you're not getting enough…"

I'm not sure what I was going to say, but her nephew who was also staying there, he was laughing away. And, as Mrs. Beyers was sort of blushing, Mel told both of us to shut up and be quiet.

She didn't bother me after that.

COLD LAKE AIR BASE

Cold lake Air Base was my first location for training in the electrical trade with Sunley Electric. We were put up in bunk houses built out of plywood floors and walls four feet high and canvas up to 8 feet high and canvas roofs. A large washroom was centrally located to serve all the workers. It was comfortable enough but not at all sound proof.

It was rough and cold and everything, but it was a good place to be. For the first time I was able to meet people my age with the same interests, goals and many with the same background. Work was not too physically hard but we were expected to be productive at all times. There was a crew of about 12 with one man in charge. The shop was strictly non-union and most of us were from the farm or from Austria and needless to say did not know the first thing about unions.

We worked extra hours at straight pay and thought we were making terrific wages. After about a year a crew from a Regina contractor moved in to do the electrical on the big cantilever hangers. They, being union, soon informed us how badly we were being abused.

Sunley had us paying for our room and board that he kept for himself, which didn't leave us with much. But, room and board was provided by the general contractor and he was pocketing that too. The apprentices, mostly 1st year, outnumbered the journeymen about 4:1 when it should have been 2:1. Over 8 hours a day work should have been paid at time and a half, and also our probation period at a lower pay (0.67$ instead of 0.96$ for beginners) should have been 3 months not 12 months. All that abuse soon came to an end but there was never any retroactive (back pay) made active.

There was one guy in charge, the foreman Al Wigglesworth, had each one of us working a different job. He would pick us up with the company truck after breakfast and take us to the shop where we would gather the tools and materials needed for our individual jobs and ask whatever we needed to know, then drive us to our sites and check things over. At lunch, he'd come by and pick us up again and we'd go through the same process.

My project was the guard house, about the size of our kitchen and hallway. Ray Faulkner had the school house and Forrest had a living complex. The others worked in pairs on the bigger buildings. It was a real hands-on rapid bit of learning.

It was a good experience, the foreman, Allan Wigglesworth was real knowledgeable and helpful, but he knew all along what Stan Sunley was doing to us and didn't do anything about it. His nickname was Wigglesbottom.

The two from Austria, Joe Mesmer and Walter Nachbar, they were good workers but getting underpaid because they weren't Canadian. But you didn't want to party with Joe. After a few drinks he became a Nazi. Yes, literally. You can tell he had been brainwashed as a kid. I don't know what experience he had. He wouldn't talk about it, but he became quite hateful when he would drink.

~~~

One time my chum and I stopped at a restaurant in Grand Centre on our way home from church. I ordered a piece of apple pie. When it was delivered, I discovered that there were mouse droppings on it. I complained to the waitress about it. She denied it and so I asked her to take a bite out of it. She wouldn't. She wouldn't replace it either.

~~~

Another experience that was awful was when Al Wigglesworth took us fishing on Cold Lake. That was fun, because the fishing was real good. It was a big rented boat and there must have been five of us at least having a great time. But, after a few drinks Al and his chum got a little reckless. He threw his line too freely and the line caught Al's wife on the lip. We didn't have any tools to get it out so we had to get to shore in a hurry.

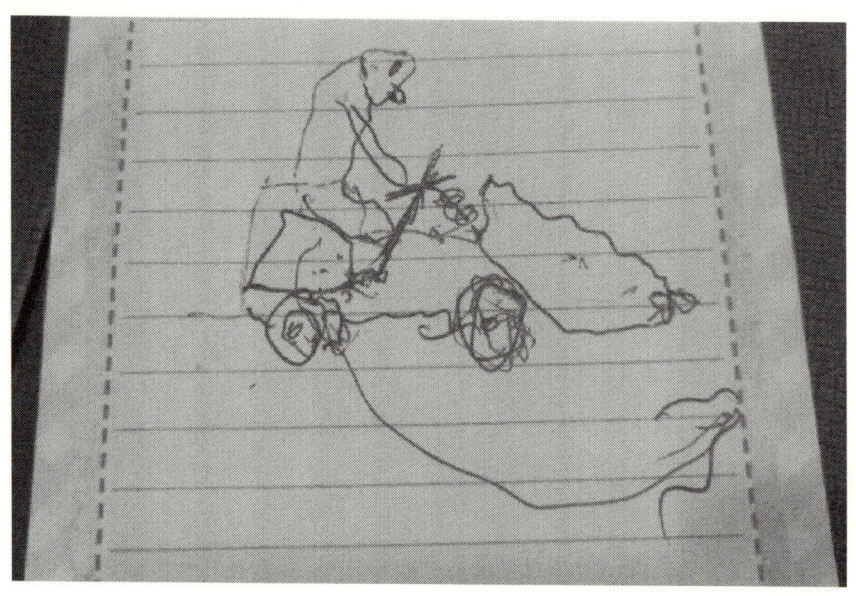

~~~

One Sunday afternoon Ray Fulkner and I walked around the hangers and found two power cement power buggies with keys in the ignition. We each got in one and we raced around the tarmac doing wheelies. Sure enough Ray tipped his over, almost getting pinned under it. But, we were able to upturn it and race home in a hurry.

You never see those again because they pump all the cement. There was a cement bucket up front on top of two wheels. In the back the two wheels were much closer together and the motor was above them and you sat on top of that. The steering turned the back two tires. You could have the front wheels sitting solid and swing the arse end around one way or the other. It was lots of fun!

BACK TO EDMONTON, 1955

After being at Cold Lake Airport for about 1 ½ years I was back at Edmonton and back to my room and board with the Beyers. My Mercury was still parked in the street after all that time.

~~~

I was still with Sunley Electric doing electrical renovations in a downtown Birks jewelry store. After about two weeks I had to change a pot-light in the ceiling over a showcase filled with expensive jewelry. I wanted to cover the case with a sheet of plywood but the boss Jack Statum said no way. He was Stan Sunley's favourite foreman. Whatever Stan said Jack did it.

I proceed to set up a 12 foot step ladder over the showcase and I went up shaking nervously. Sure enough reaching into the confined space of this pot-light I lost my grip on the screw driver which hit the edge of the plate-glass top which in turn split down the middle and fell into the precious display.

Years later, the strange thing about it, when the foothills hospital was first built, Sunley Electric had the contract, and Jack was in charge there. I was thinking of meeting him to talk things over but when I checked he had already died of a heart attack.

~~~

I gotta tell you about when I got electrocuted. ("Which time was that?" they asked in unison) I was a First year apprentice; I think it was at the university. I was told to go in a tunnel with a cord and an electric hammer and told to drill a hole through the end of the tunnel to run a conduit through. So, I went in there dragging the cord, and the light and the drill, in this little tunnel that was only about 3' x 3' with water pipes and all kinds of pipes lining the walls. I got into position; I was laying down and drilling and I moved a bit and got my neck against a water pipe and got a shock.

At that time the electric drills weren't isolated. They're supposed to have a proper ground wire, but apparently this one wasn't grounded. It got to me to the extent that I couldn't release the switch. My eyesight went first. I blacked out and couldn't see a thing, then my hearing and eventually I collapsed. I was thinking I was a dead man. But, when I collapsed, my finger let go and I was out.

Because I was young and healthy, my heart started pumping again, I guess it hadn't stopped all together but I came back to wondering where the hell I was. You could say I came out of the tunnel kinda mad. The foreman just laughed about it and told me to go back to work, but fortunately he gave me something else to do. I seriously considered quitting the trade. It was too dangerous.

~~~

Another first year experience, I was told to meet my journeyman at a house at a certain address. Of course, I was there early. But, the journeyman didn't show up. Eventually the woman came out, a pretty young thing in her night gown. We talked for a while. I told her my journeyman was coming. She said she had a problem that I could fix. I asked what it was and she said, "My electric blanket isn't working."

I think I stammered for a while and blushed. Eventually I figured maybe she was telling the truth and I figured I was big enough to defend myself against her if I had to. So I went in there and sure enough her electric blanket wasn't working, but I don't think I was able to fix it. I was able to get out of there in quite a hurry.

URANIUM CITY

Our living quarters and kitchen was about a mile from the mill. There used to be bus service, but you had to have breakfast in a hurry if you woke up late in order to catch the bus. One morning two of us missed the bus. We decided to walk. But, it was so cold and windy that even with our parka hoods up, we ended up walking the distance backwards.

~~~

Before all this, when we flew up there we were in a DC3 freight airplane and we had to sit on canvas seats along the side wall in amongst the freight. It was cold, but finally we were coming in for a landing. As we were approaching the runway, the pilot revved up the engine and lifted again. When we looked out the window, we could see there was another plane already on the runway.

When we finally came back for a landing we could see down below that there was the wreckage of a DC3 just before the approach to the landing strip which was on a plateau. So it was quite the experience.

~~~

Eventually we fitted into the routine and our foreman was Grant Miller, a cocky character but not too experienced. They had us erecting the towers for the substations, which measured about 10 feet by 20 and about 30 feet high. It too was quite the experience because we weren't steel riggers. When we had the first one done they came along with a mobile crane to put the insulators and other electrical stuff on to the tower. I said to Grant, "This is kind of backwards."

He said something to the idea of, ya ok smart ass, what would you do? So I said, "Since this big crane is available, let's assemble all of that steel on the ground! We can reach everything with a ladder. Once the steel is erected, we can put the insulators on, and then bring the crane and lift the whole thing up."

He figured it was a good idea. He went to his boss about it and sure enough they agreed. We ended up putting the next two towers up in less than half the time.

That was a prime example of teaching superiors how to do things right.

But, I'm sure he went to his boss taking credit for the idea.

~~~

Summer time Uranium city, I was in charge of delivering material to the different tower locations; the insulators and whatnot. I had a private chauffer. Because of the union, I wasn't allowed to drive. The driver was quite interesting. He didn't have any schooling at all. In grade one he got sick and couldn't finish. In grade 2 he went back to school but because he was bigger than all the other kids, so he quit.

Lots of this material we couldn't deliver right up to the site, so we had to deliver it by hand. When it came time to pull in the wires over these small mountains they had all these guys lined up about 100 feet apart holding the wires on their shoulder and slowly trudging up the mountain. I figured that was too much like slave labour. Once again they asked, "What would you do?"

I said, "Well we've got a truck with a winch, all we need is a quarter inch cable about 500 feet long. That way we can pull all four wires at once. All we need to do is get the cable over the mountain to the truck and then at the end tie the wires together."

They rebutted, "We can't drag the aluminum over the rocks."

I said, "Do the same as before. Space your men 100 feet apart and haul all four wires on their shoulder and we'll do the pulling with the winch."

They look surprised and said, "Good idea!"

So, that's what they did! Once again, much easier and much faster.

~~~

I think I was up there twice. I think it was a year and half all together.

~~~

The one bad experience was when they asked me to wire three different houses that were newly built and I volunteered. It was right next to Beaver Lake in the summer and the sand flies were attracted to the lumber. In no time at all they were biting me all over the place. And then, the worst thing about it is that they would get in behind my glasses and instead of finding their way out they would fly straight into my eyes! By the third day, I couldn't open my eyes because they were swollen shut. After a week or so, I went back to the mill but then they had two journeymen working nights wiring the houses. I was sort of disappointed that they got the extra time and money and they hadn't asked me. They sent me back to the mill, because of the noise and the stink, the sand flies didn't bother anyone there.

~~~

Sometimes on a Sunday afternoon the surveyor, who had a company vehicle, would go driving in the community and a few times I would go with him. One Sunday he decided to go meet a friend on the reservation. Sure enough his friend had been drinking along with his wife. The woman came out and wanted scotch or rum, I don't remember but she wanted a drink and we didn't have any, but she wanted us to get some. We wouldn't do it, so she offered us her daughter in exchange. We drove away from there in quite a hurry.

~~~

The one entertainment that we did have was when, my buddy Forrest Boyles and I would have shooting matches. We had those high powered guns to shoot pins into cement or steel. We discovered that if we put a welding rod in the guns that we could shoot those. So we were shooting welding rods at each other.

We made sure we stayed a safe distance apart and that we could see them coming at us. And, of course we had coveralls on.

~~~

When I first got up there I used to hitch hike up to Uranium city with whoever was going to church, but eventually it got to be quite the chore to find someone who was going to church. There were no taxis available. Finally I went to confession and told the priest I was missing mass quite often. And he asked me, "Why did you come up here, to work or to go to mass?"

I answered, "To work."

He asked how long I planned on being there. I said, "Well, one year at the most."

And, he said, "Well then go to work."

I did, but in the meantime, it got easier not going to mass or even saying prayers, but I did eventually return to Edmonton.

EDMONTON

Shortly after being back in Edmonton, they sent me along with Rod MacDonald, I was a fourth year apprentice and on a Sunday night we were told to be at the municipal airport to go up to Fort Smith. We ended up in a little Cessna with Rod sitting up front with the pilot and I sat in the back with the tools and materials. We no sooner took off that the pilot was fidgeting and sweating. He turned the plane around. I asked him what was wrong. He wouldn't say. He didn't even have contact with the airport.

We found out after we landed that we didn't have any oil pressure. We were lucky that there wasn't anyone on the runway when we had to make our emergency landing.

We went back home and around 9 o'clock we got a call to go back to the airport. We did and we landed at Ft. McMurray, but there was nothing up there then. From there we went up to Fort Smith in the North West Territories.

There was a company from Truckee California that was moving their lumber mill all the way from California to Fort Fitzgerald. By the time they got there everything was covered in dust, even the electrical stuff. There were all kinds of problems because of the dust. After we got a few things going with the two diesel power plants, that supplied the lights at nights, but they were mainly for operating the compressors so they could operate the jack hammers to break up the rocks to prepare for building. After two weeks Rod MacDonald went back to Edmonton and I was up there all alone. I was the only electrician up there and I had all sorts of problems. I would contact the office on some sort of radio; it wasn't a regular phone. Every time I called I wouldn't get George Saunders, the superintendent. I would get the estimator and I would order different things but I would never hear back. Finally things got so badly out of hand that I quit. When I got back to the office at Wirtanen Electric, George Saunders was there and he asked, "What are you doing here?"

I said, "I quit. Nothing was going right."

He asked, "Why didn't you tell me?"

I said, "I tried! You weren't here."

He said, "I was on holidays."

I thought, "Big hairy deal!"

He asked, "You realize you're fired?"

I said, "I'm not fired. I quit!"

They were hoping for a hell of a lot from an apprentice! They had been good to me, but that was kind of rough.

In fact, when I started with them I was asked to wire an open air hockey rink which was George Saunders' community rink. That was quite different. I had never seen a hockey rink wired before! There were lights in the shack and over the rink.

~~~

Fort Smith was the last place and that's when I decided to go to California. That had to be in 56. But then I stopped here in Calgary to go to the embassy I was going to go to Anaheim to visit my cousin, Terry Pugh. Then I was informed at the embassy that if I went to the states I'd most likely be conscripted to go fight in Korea.

So then I decided I better stay in Calgary for a year or so until I was too old to be conscripted. And then all hell broke loose.

That was the one good thing about the Korean War is that the kids wouldn't be here if it wasn't for that.

That's it. You know what happened after that. You've heard it all before.

And, then Michelle talked me into saying more.

CALGARY

I got a job with Hume & Rumble working night shift at the Hudson Bay store. That's when they added three more floors to the building. A good friend of mine, Bill Robertson, that I would go pheasant hunting with informed me that his wife was working at the Holy Cross hospital, there were two young nurses from Toronto who wanted dates for New Year's. I, along with another guy, volunteered to be blind dates. We made arrangements to go to a movie before New Year's. It was December 6. When I showed up in Mount Royal, my buddy didn't show up. I thought I would have to decide between these two beauties, but as it turned out they decided for me and it turned out for the best, for sure!

~~~

Paul, "But, just to put me to the test, Mary-Adele bashed my head into a window"

"Oh that was much later." says Mary-Adele. "Dec 6, 1959 it was the Feast of St. Nikolas. Paul and I met on a blind date. He was tall, dark, good looking, and dressed meticulously in a white shirt, dark tie, charcoal grey suit and a grey top coat. He wasn't sure whether he was dating Marion, my roommate or me! I said it was going to be me!

We went to the show to see The Hunch Back of Notre Dame. I had my eyes shut through a lot of it. After, we went for coffee then home. He was very polite. And, I told him I liked skiing, he was willing to go skiing, he didn't know how, but he wanted to go. So, we arranged to go the following week, Saturday. The three of us Marion, Paul and I went up to Mt. Norquay, skied all day and had a ball. That night he had a date with another woman; he took her to a movie and fell asleep.

He came over the next week in the evening and we played cards.

From then on he came over every day, and we played cards, wrote letters home, listened to music and played bridge with the neighbours Arne and Lorraine Fors, And after 6 weeks of this, he proposed."

Paul, "She didn't say no."

"No! I put him off. I told him to go ask my father. I didn't want to lose him, but I wasn't ready to say yes." She admits. "He was catholic, and he had the same missal (for church) as I had which was very unusual. And, it had the mass for Our Lady of Good Council, who was my patron saint. He wasn't' a big spender and I knew he had money in the bank. And, he had a car."

Paul, "Actually, my money was in the car. It was in the glove compartment on our first date and I was worried she was going to steal it."

"In March, I flew home to Toronto, and my mother Kathleen asked if there was anything serious between Paul and me. I shyly answered, 'kind of...'.

He had phoned my father while Jay and Jocelyn where listening behind.

When I got back he gave me my ring in May and we had Bill Brownridge design the wedding ring. I didn't want any diamonds in it as I'd be wearing to work. (I assume that lowered the price substantially as well, which should have made Dad happy.)

In the meanwhile, we had gone to the farm to visit his family. We drove up to Edmonton on the weekend. We left after work so we didn't get there until after 12:00. We went into a hotel and got two rooms, then I said, This is stupid, we're going to get up at 6 o'clock in the morning to leave. What are we paying all this money for? Surely there's a cheaper place around. So, we went back and got our money and he knew of a place that was just rooms with the bathroom in the hallway, which was fine in those days.

We stayed for the night and headed out to the farm. I stayed with Helen and tried to speak to his mom although I didn't have enough French and his mother wouldn't speak English for being embarrassed.

In September my father came out with Kathleen to check Paul out. They stayed with Marion and me. They liked Paul and had a good visit with us.

In the end everyone approved and Dad and Kathleen organized everything. We didn't have to think of a thing. Other than, I bought the dress in Calgary.

Paul flew out and he stayed with Dave and Isabel Ramsey. That's Kathleen's brother and his wife in their hotel room and watched TV.

We were married by Monsignor Doyle at Our Lady of Perpetual Help. He was at the reception too. Father Bill O'Brien was there with his sister Kathleen O'Brien who was my bridesmaid. George Nedelec was Paul's best man and Bert Malhome, George's friend was there. The reception was held, at I can't remember the name, was it Clarendon House near Casa Loma? It was an old beautiful home. All my family was there; my cousins, Aunty Marjorie, Joan came from Ottawa. Helen O'Kelly, Bob and Sharron, and Carolyn came.

After the reception I said, You should really phone your mom and dad. 'Cause we really hadn't talked to any of them…Where did we leave George? Oh ya, and Bert?"

Paul, "We didn't really worry about them too much. "

"Oh I think my brother took them to Casa Loma or something."

Paul, "Is that right?"

"Ya, I think so. He wasn't too concerned about calling his parents either. The wedding was in the morning and the reception in the early afternoon so they would have been awake; it was only an hour's difference. Finally he did and there wasn't any enthusiasm.

My father had people over after the reception and we went over to visit them for a while.

We had a motel in Richmond Hill, and then we went up to Collingwood to ski. When we got there we saw that the whole hill was ice cubes! Great big ice cubes. It was terrible. They had broken up the ice on the hill and it was just a mess! It just so happened that Arne and Lorraine were staying at a place nearby so we spent the week playing bridge with Arne and Lorraine.

Someone had done the reservation, I don't know who, but the beds were bunk bed cots on the wall! We, of course, were too embarrassed to ask for another room."

Paul, "We should have only paid ½ price because we only ever used one bed."

"We went back to Toronto where we met back up with Arne and Lorraine to take us back to Calgary. They had their cat,"

Paul, "Bones,"

"in the car with us. Every once in a while they needed to let Bones out to do his job. One night it was miserable! I guess it was just outside of Winnipeg or some place. It was bitterly cold, Arne let him out, and the darn cat wouldn't come back. Finally Arne went after it to bring back this stupid cat. He was not happy. And, he was the one driving the WHOLE way back. We didn't mind any of it. We sat in the back necking."

Paul, "I don't remember paying them for gas or anything."

~~~

When we got back to Calgary, I was so excited because I had bought so many things for my new bride! A vacuum cleaner…,and all sorts of different things for the apartment. When I checked to see where the stuff was the guy said, "We don't have any record here. Who did you buy from?"

So I told him and he says, "Well, he's no longer with us."

I said, "Give me his address and phone number at least."

I finally contacted him, but he wouldn't talk to me so I tried again, and he still wouldn't talk to me. So I went to work at 7am at that time, and I headed out early and banged on his door at about 6 o'clock. Finally he gave in and answered the door. I told him I want the stuff or the money. He had all sorts of excuses that he was out of work, etc. I said, "That's kinda rough. But, I want my stuff!"

There was a whole list of stuff; a vacuum, a sewing machine, every time I turned something down he'd add something else to the list.

Finally I agreed to take 10 postdated cheques. I said, "If they bounce, I'll be back at 6 in the morning again."

They didn't bounce.

~~~

My good friend Forrest Boyles, we worked together at Cold Lake and Uranium City, when we came back to Edmonton, he got engaged to his high school girlfriend. He wanted to get married, but couldn't afford it. He spent it as soon as he got it. So, I lent him some money and I was his best man. And then, I didn't hear from him. Finally I tracked him down and told him I wanted the money. He said, "Oh we're trying to buy furniture and different things. I can't afford it."

I said, "There's no darn way I'm going to be paying for your fun! I want money!"

So once again, I agreed to postdated cheques. I think I extended it over two years. I finally got it, but then the friendship was up. I moved to Calgary, and before I knew it, he was here in Calgary as well. I couldn't get rid of him! He was a disaster. After a few experiences like that and you learn you can't trust anybody.

~~~

When we first came back we were living in Marda Loop and Mary-Adele was working nights. "I was no good working nights," she adds. "I'd fall asleep at 4 in the morning or so and I was just exhausted all the time. Never really getting enough sleep."

Paul; "Not a very exciting Bride!"

"Oh I was as owly as could be. I could barely survive."

"I figured, 'What had I married!?!?"

"He was ready to leave and think things over. Finally, I got off nights and I was a different person. It was awful."

~~~

One time we were living in Marda Loop with quite a nice couple, but he used to drink quite a bit. This one night Marion and Ed Svenson were over playing cards with us. This landlord comes in to our basement suite, obviously drunk, and he asked for help. His car was stuck. So we asked him where and he said, "In the front yard." He had driven right up into the hedges.

~~~

After Marda Loop we moved to this place on 11th street south west. "Paul took me to the hospital in the morning to deliver Ann-Marie. Kathleen O'Bryan, was an air stewardess, came to Calgary to visit. Paul in the morning, he drove to work and took Kathleen with him. She had to drive the car back, but she didn't really know where it was. Resourcefully, she got a cab to take her back! She followed him with the car.

At work the guys saw me with her in the car. One guy even approached me and asked, "I thought your wife was pregnant?"

"Yes," I said, "She's in the hospital delivering right now!" They figured I was a pretty fast operator.

When I got home the landlady was wondering where Mary-Adele was. She was likely curious as Kathleen was there, spending the nights over and all. I said she was in the hospital delivering and left it at that. Who knows, what she was thinking.

~~~

Not too long after, Mary-Adele's father and Kathleen came

out for Ann-Marie's christening. Helen, My sister and Mary-Adele's brother were the godparents. They didn't do much for her, but then I guess I didn't do much either. I'm a godfather to Annette Wolford and Nancy Reed. They turned out all right.

~~~

One time Mary-Adele locked herself out. There was no door between our place and the lady downstairs, it was just a staircase. She went out and I was outside hanging the wash. Ann-Marie was a baby. She was in her bassinet sleeping. "And, I was BIG!" Mary-Adele adds, "It wasn't too long before she was born. There was a ladder against the house but I didn't know how strong it was. There was a big man, really heavy, and I asked him to help me with the ladder, which he did. But, he said he wasn't going up it, he was too heavy. So, there I am going up the ladder. Hating it! I'm terrified of heights. I got up to the window, it was open so I was able to open it up completely, and got in. "She tumbled in! Headfirst! But she got in before Ann-Marie woke up.

~~~

We flooded the place twice. We had our washing machine upstairs with us, and water went through the floor twice!

~~~

Did I tell you about the time that I had stomach pains at work? I had gone to work and had fantastic stomach pains, but of course I thought they would pass. They didn't pass. After lunch it hurt so bad that I decided I should see a doctor, so I drove to the hospital, where they kept poking and prodding and it hurt. One nurse came in and asked if she could touch it and I finally said, "Only if I get to touch yours." They eventually discovered that it was my appendix. ~~~

The spring of '59 we bought east of Calgary. We looked on

the west but it was full of rocks and over $4000. We wanted to grow a garden, so that wasn't any good to us. We looked everywhere looking for anything. We found this, and we liked it so we made arrangements with the farmer. We didn't know anything back then so Mary-Adele went to the real-estate agent with $4000 cash, signed the paper, and it was OUR LAND!

We'd drive out and park on the dirt road out front. We planted a garden up at the front. I think it was the same year; we got Danny Kelly to come help us out. He was a teenager and a big guy. Mary-Adele at 8 1/5 months pregnant and Danny would clean up the land so we could plant a garden, and move the rocks to the middle of the property to build the foundation for the driveway. Mary-Adele would lift the rocks and he would chase the mice. She hated mice that much. In 1961 we built the driveway.

~~~

As time flew by we had 5 children in all. And yes, it was a coincidence that they were named in alphabetical order. But it does make it easier to remember sometimes.

We now have 7 grandchildren and 2 great grandchildren. Apparently some are just grander than the others. ;)

Ann-Marie born 1960
   Wynona born 1982
      Alexzander born 2003
      Emma born 2012
   Eli born 1985
   Jan born 1987

Bernadette born 1961
   Sascha born 2001
   Mikaela born 2003
Caroline born 1963
Lawrence born 1964
   Eva born 2009
Michelle born 1970
   Beau born 1993

~~~

I retired when I was 60, and that was the day Michelle came down to surprise us! She sure did! That's how I remember how old Beau is! It was 25 years ago, and he's 24!

I'm sure glad I retired at that time. At that time my friend, Berny Botner, he was the maintenance foreman at the Convention Centre, he had prostate cancer, and died. Not long before that the neighbour over here, he retired at 65, Ralph Horning, his wife had been sick for years, but he no sooner retired then he died. His wife didn't last very long after that. I figured if I retired at 60 I might get 10 years of retirement. But now, it's been 25 years! And, going strong!

The guys would ask me at work, "What are you going to do in retirement? Where are you going?"

"I'm going to stay right where I am; that was the plan!"

They said, "Your pension will be lower!" you know, because of the fact that I'm retiring early.

I said, "Yes, but…I'll be collecting it that much longer!" It worked out. I fooled them!

EPILOGUE

So, if someone finds this book 100 years from now who never knew me, I would say this to them. Life is short so smarten up and enjoy every day as if it's your last. Loosen up. Enjoy life. Be sociable. Talk to your family. Be nice. Sit down with the people you need to sit down with and talk to them. The past is the past don't let it bugger up your future. Encourage people to talk and to enjoy life. Let people who need to talk to you, talk to you and give them the opportunity to let it go and enjoy life.

Whether you think it's exciting or dull, write your memoires for future generations. If I can do it, so can you!

ABOUT THE AUTHOR

Paul F Nedelec is the proud loving husband of Mary-Adele Nedelec, (born Mary-Adele Hodgins of Ottawa, Ontario. They have 5 adored and accomplished children, Ann-Marie, Bernadette, Caroline, Lawrence and Michelle. All of whom are blessed with wonderful spouses. Paul considers himself to be very fortunate to have 7 wonderful grandchildren, and at the writing of this book 2 great grandchildren. He loves to surround himself with family as much as he loves to putter on his farm in Calgary, Alberta

Dad was encouraged to write and publish this book in time for his 85th birthday because Michelle decided it was a great idea for the theme of his party. We thought she was being lazy making Dad do all the work for the party, but in the end it worked out all right. ;-)

We also, couldn't let it end here because we figured that you the reader should have an opportunity to see how a man who grew up with these stories would impact the world. He most certainly impacted the people in life, many of whom have passed on, many of whom he doesn't get a chance to see much of anymore and many of whom he still visits and socializes with. We gathered a few of our favourite PFN stories for you. We hope you enjoy them even though you couldn't possibly enjoy them as much as we did.

Thank you again, for being our favourite father.

From your favourite oldest daughter,
your favourite middle daughter,
your favourite daughter,
your favourite son, and
your favourite youngest daughter.
And, all your favourite grandkids and great grandkids.
And, yes, we all know Caroline was your real favourite. ☺

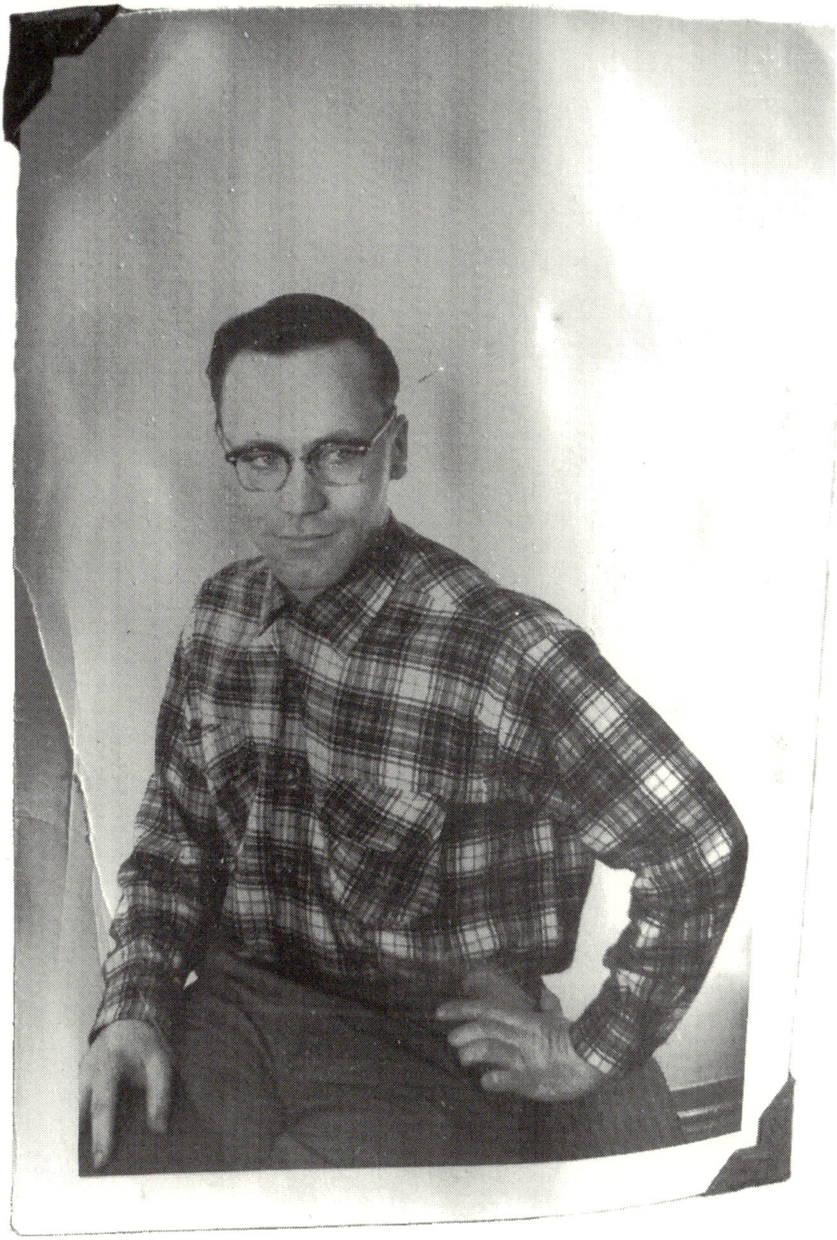

PAUL FERNAND NEDELEC

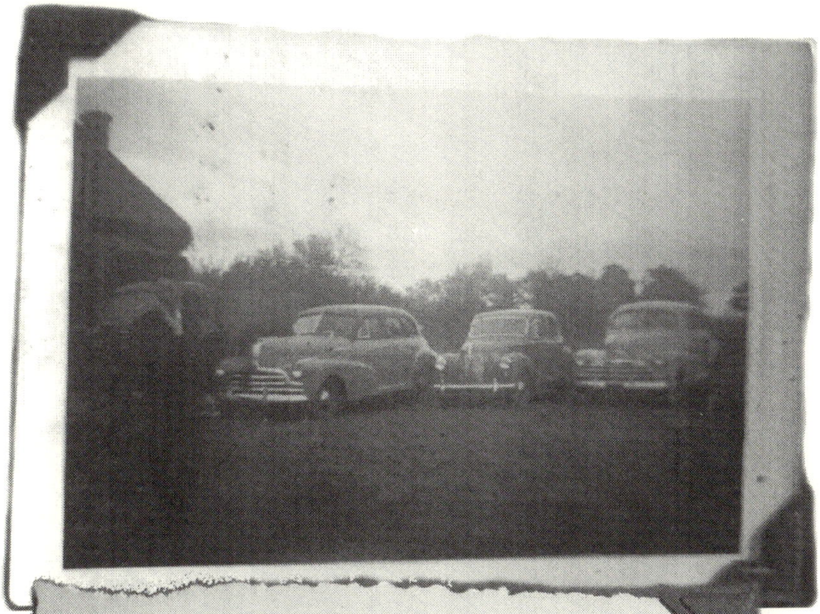

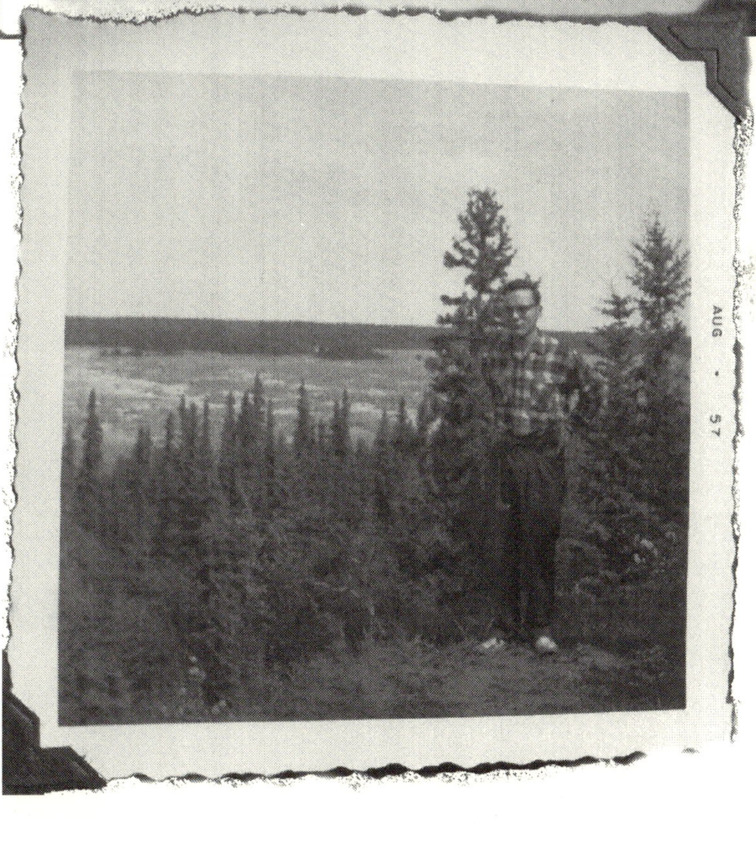
AUG • 57

PAUL FERNAND NEDELEC

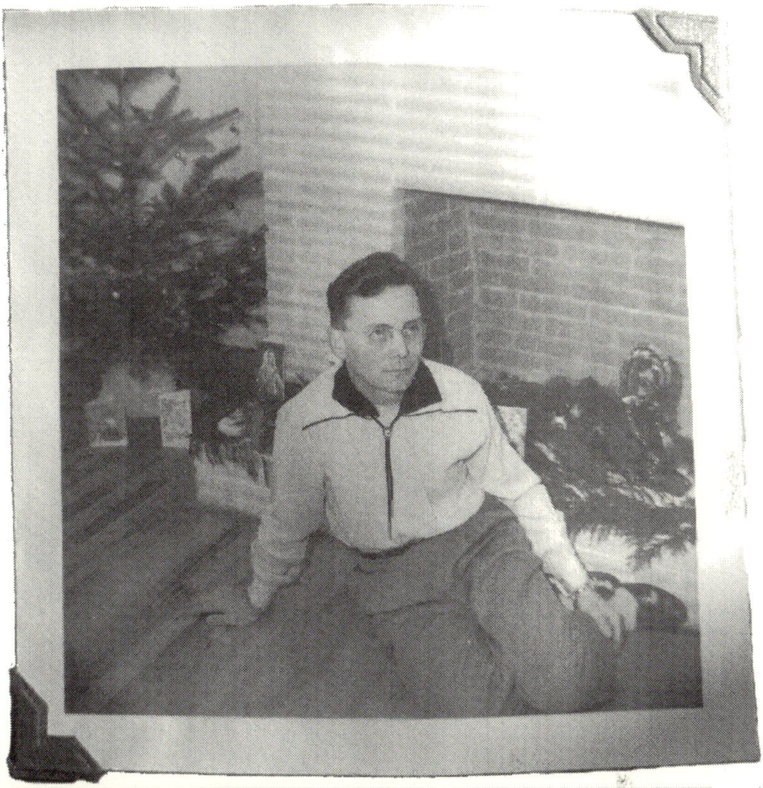

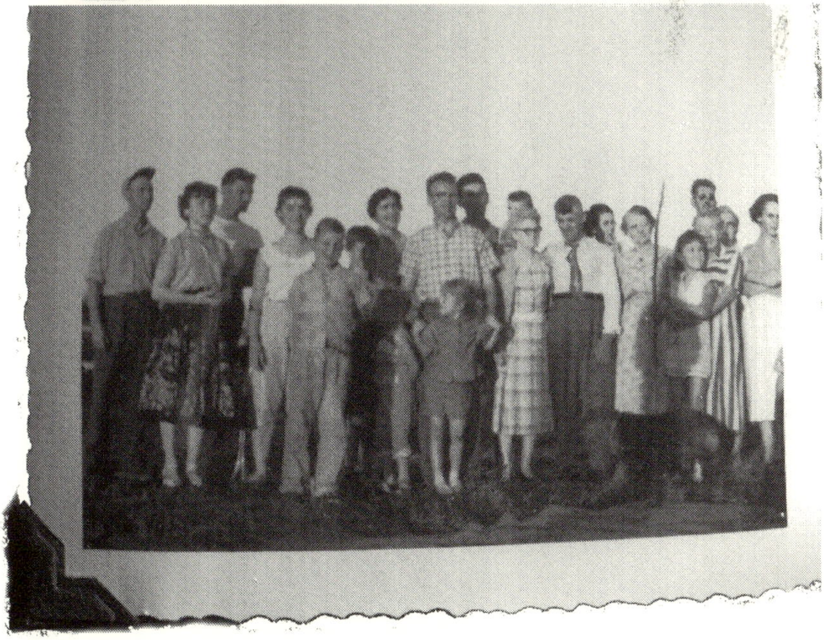

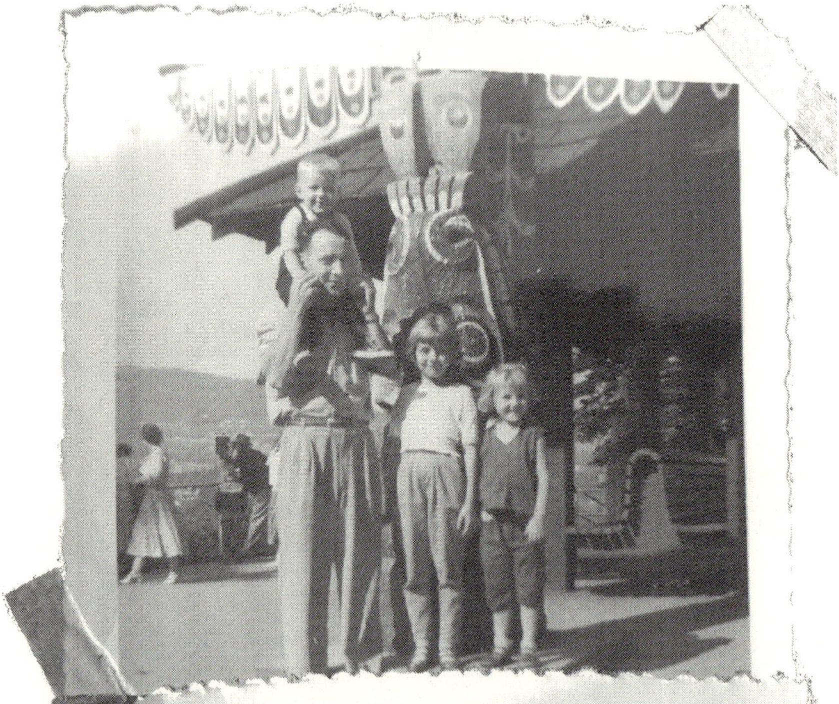

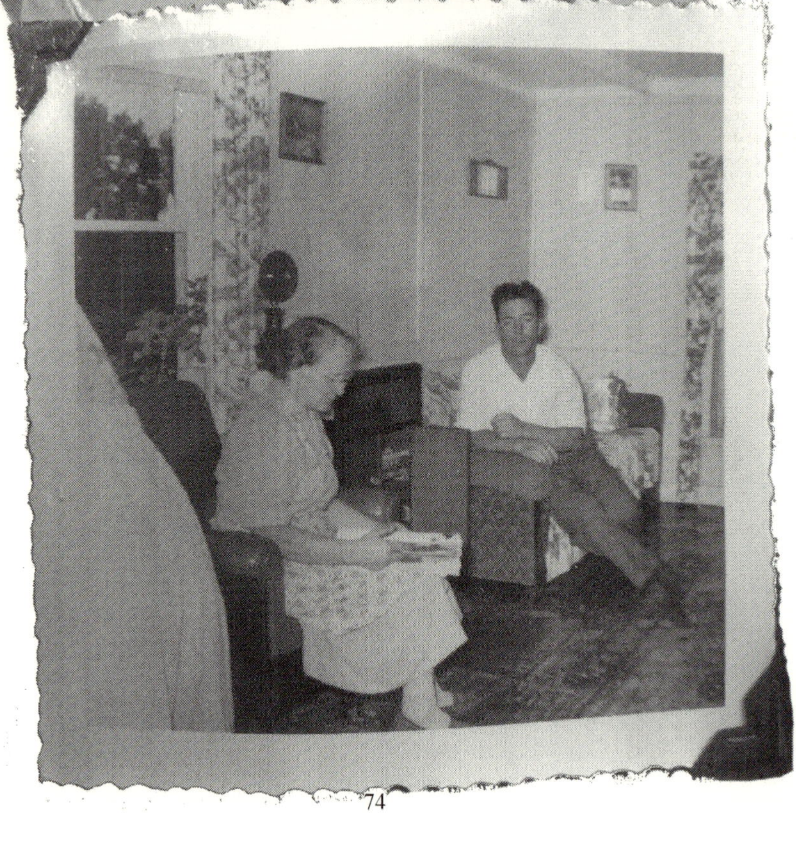

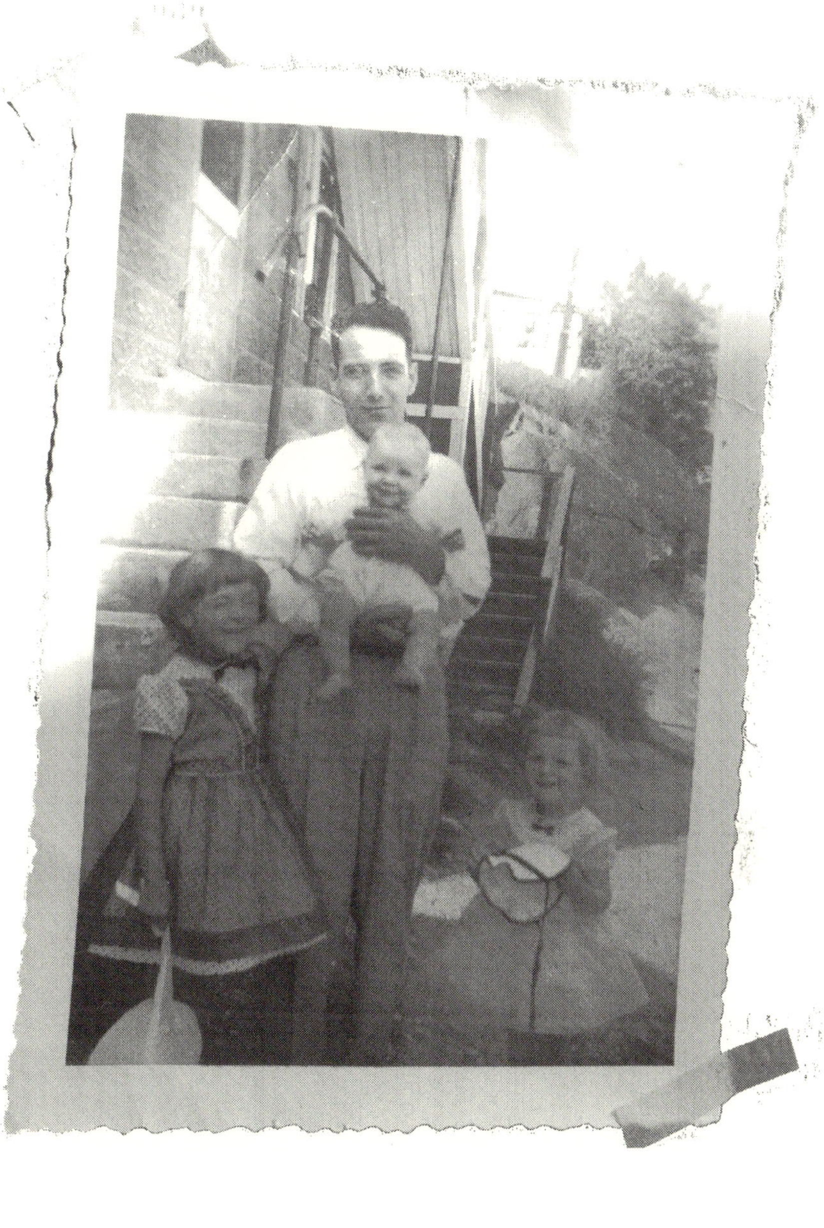

PAUL FERNAND NEDELEC

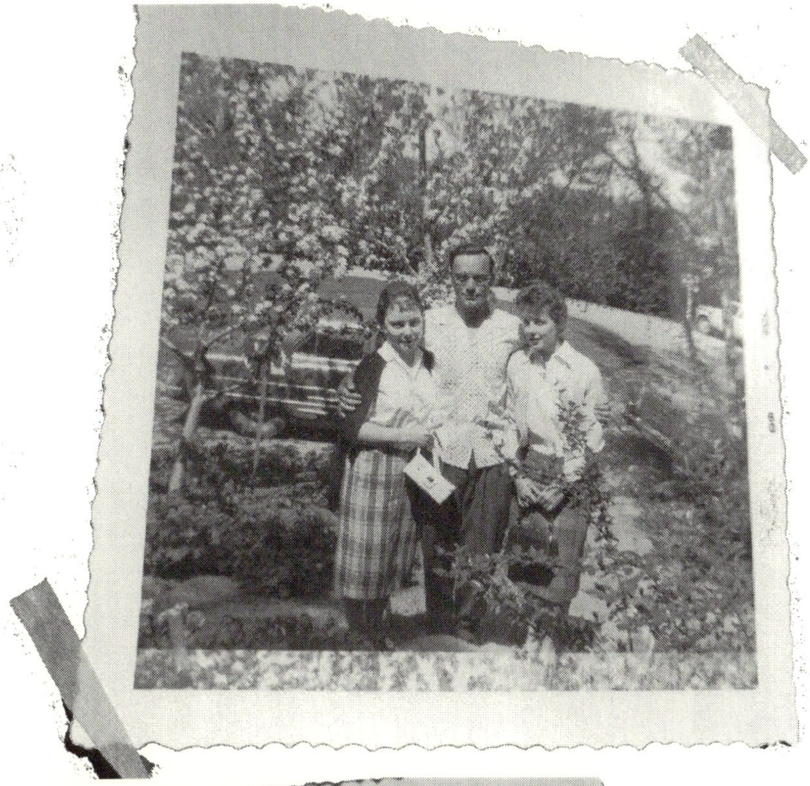

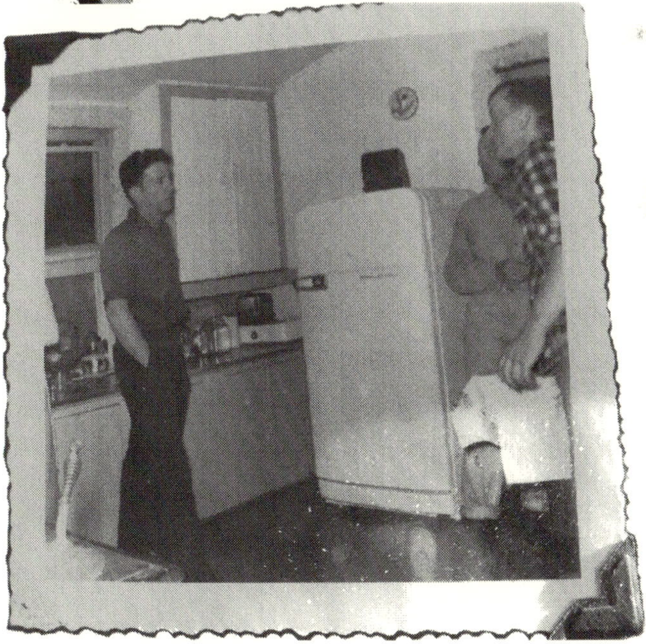

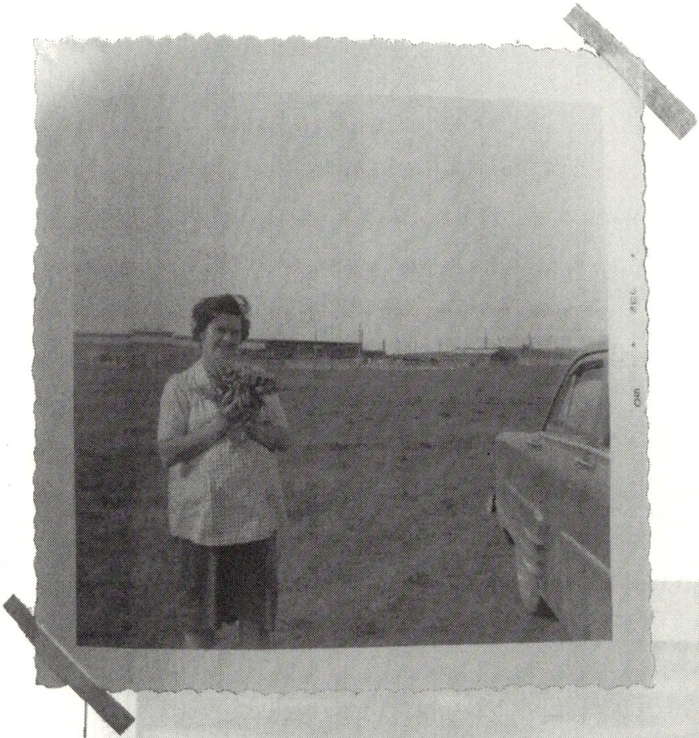

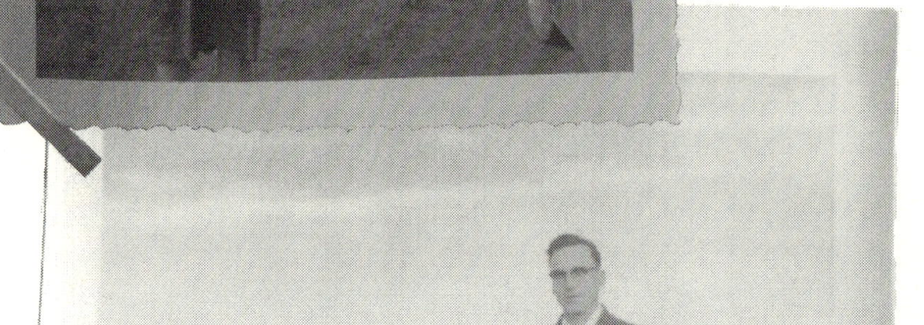

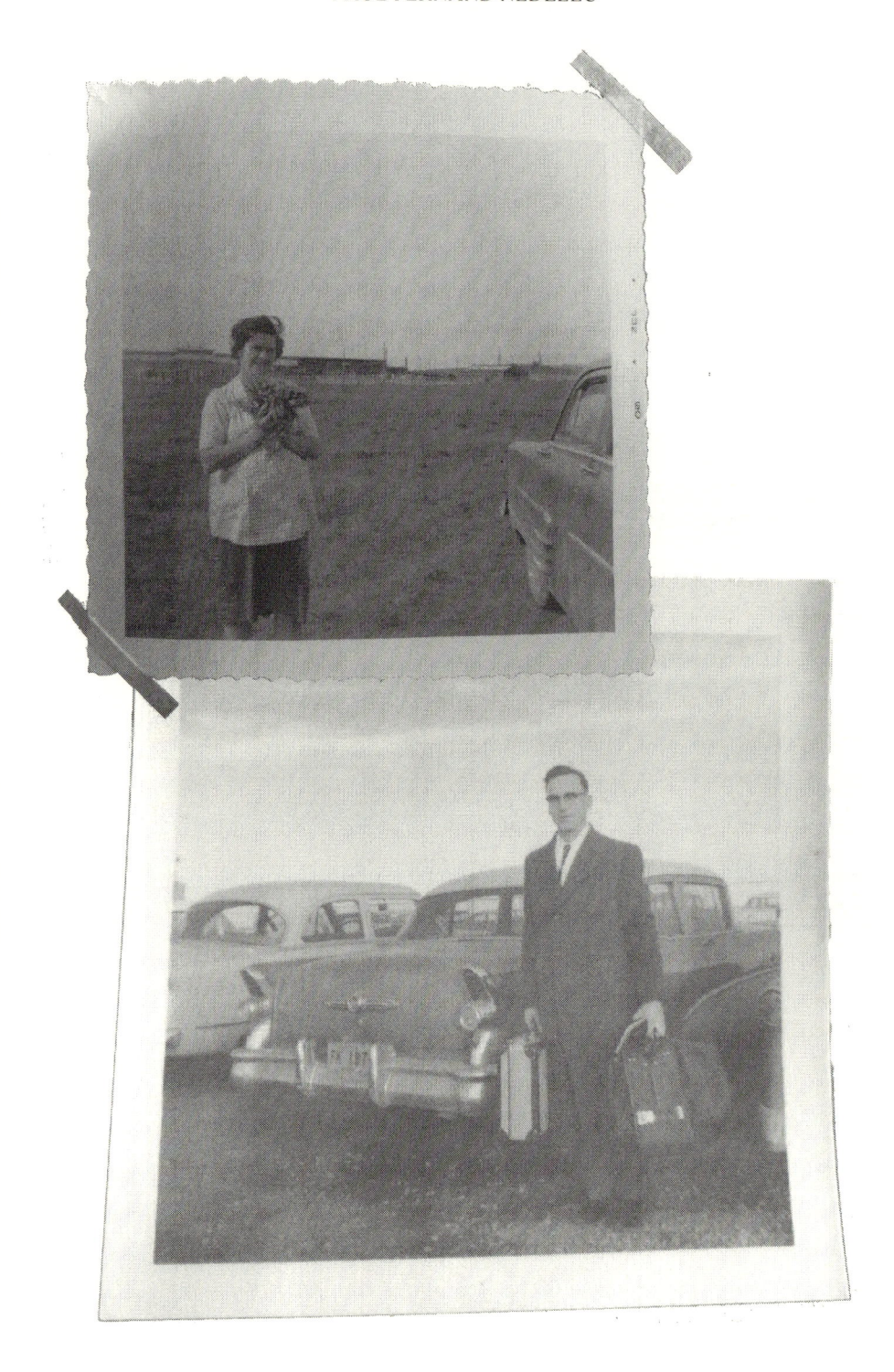

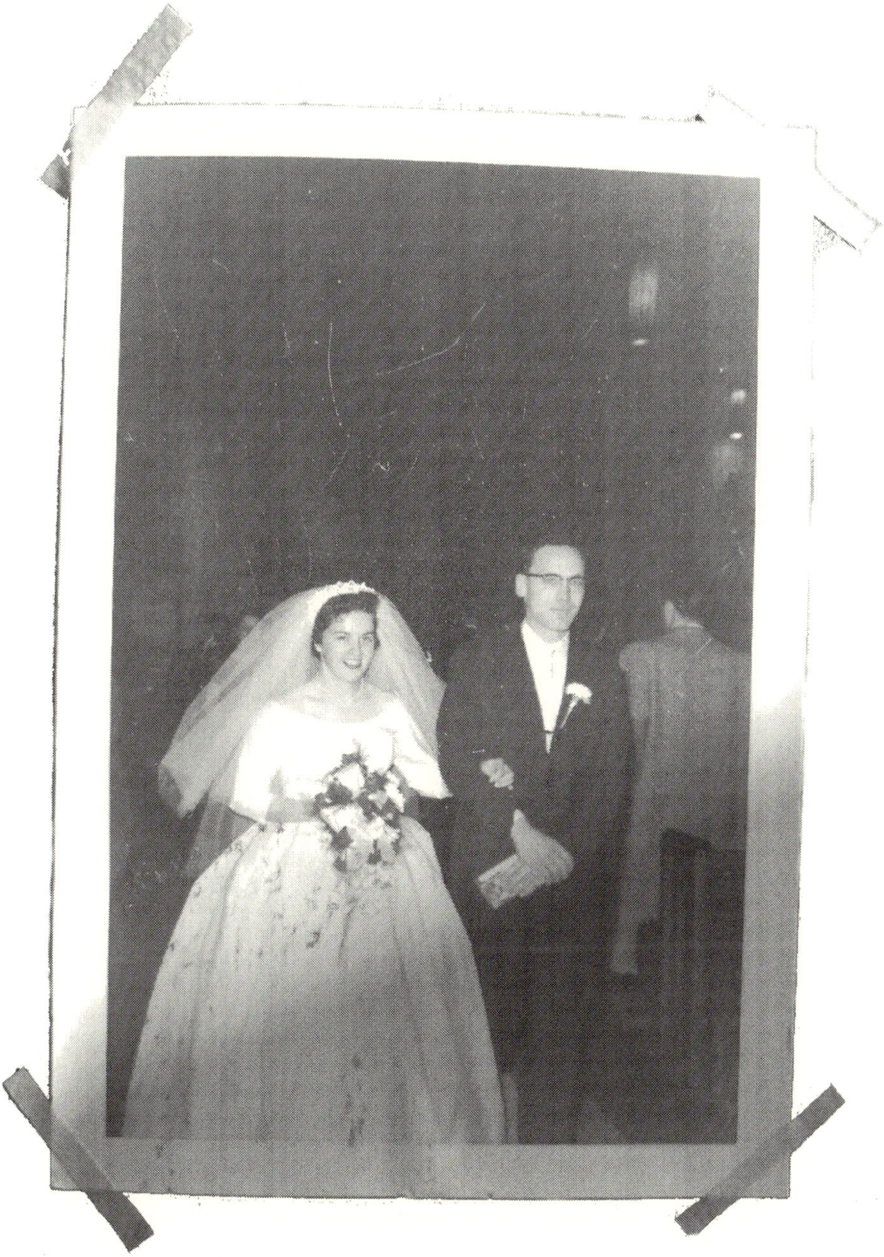

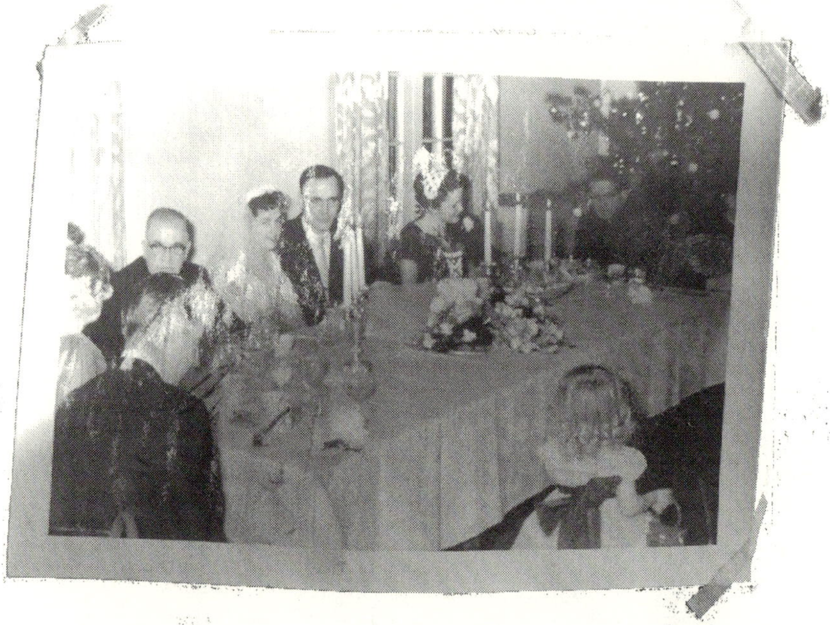

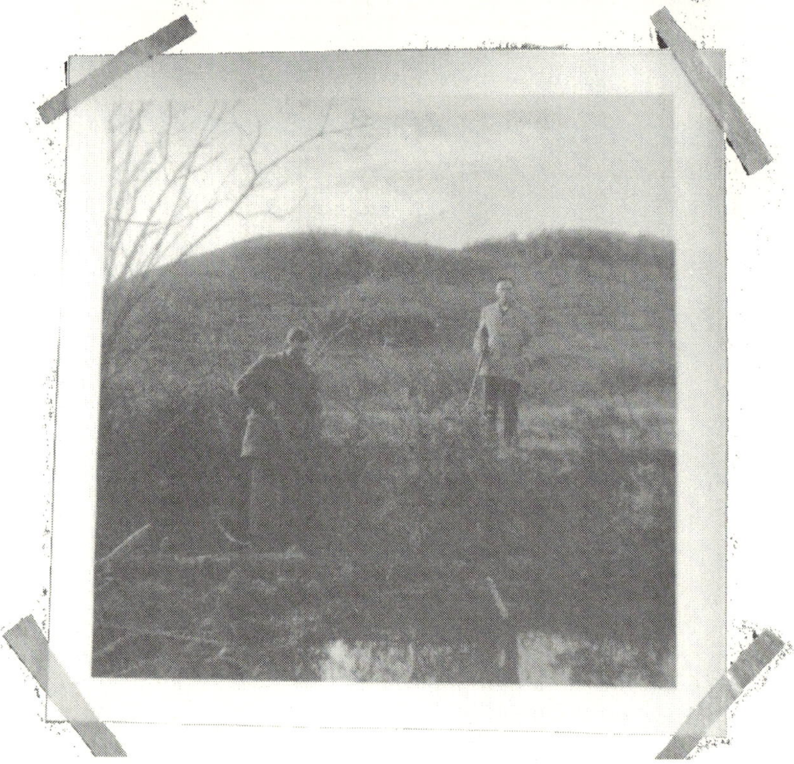

MEMOIRS OF PFN

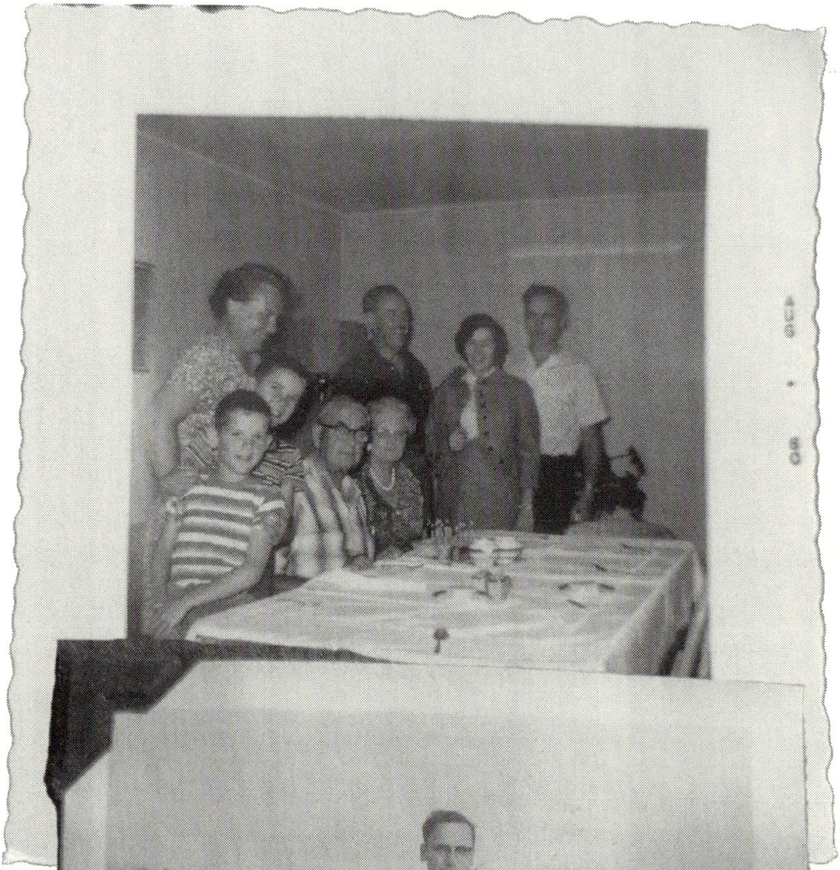

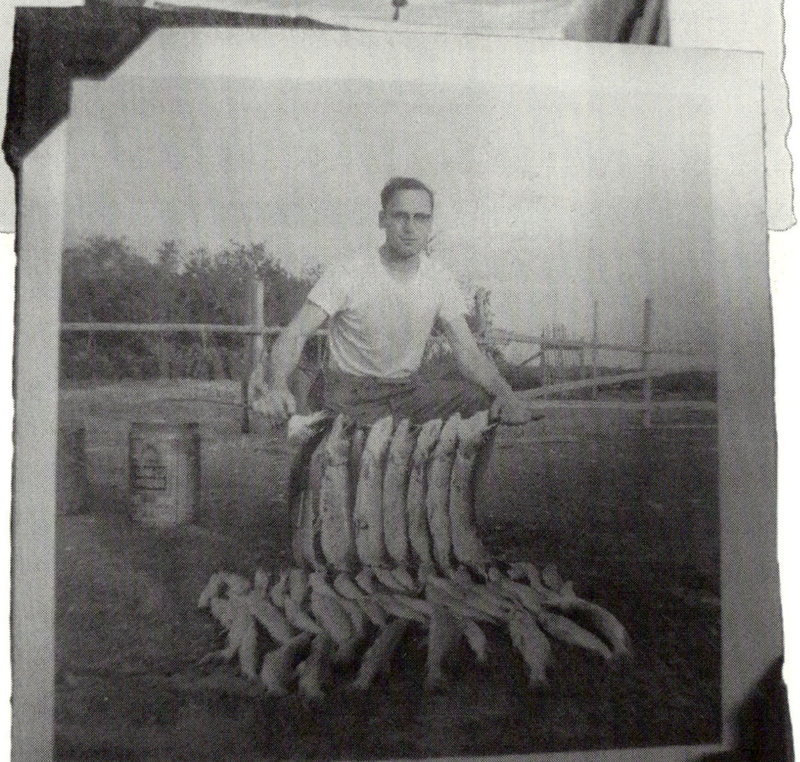

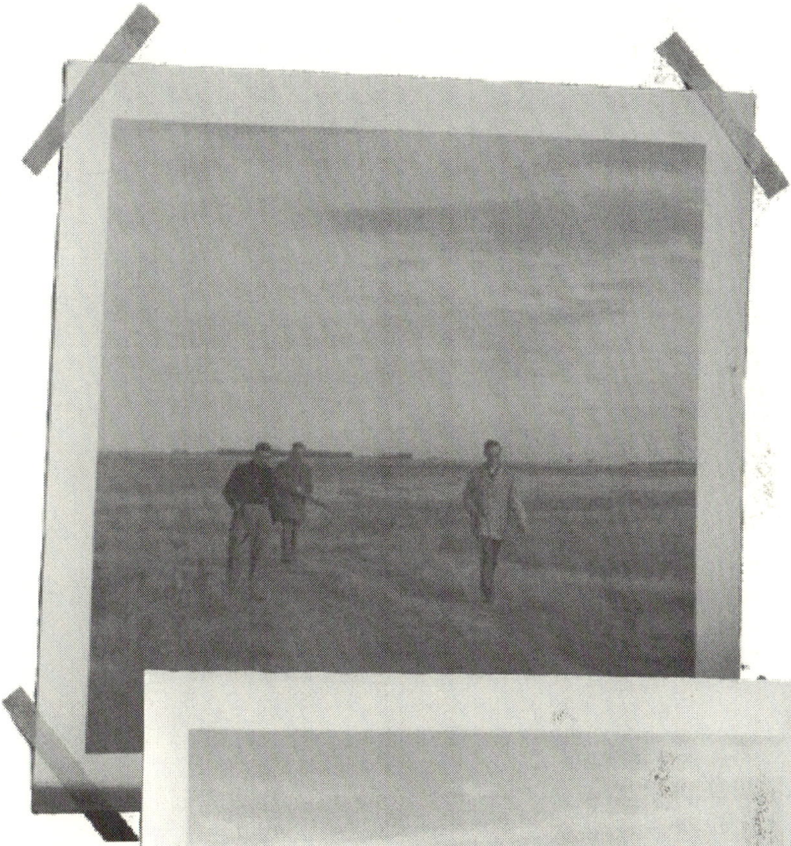

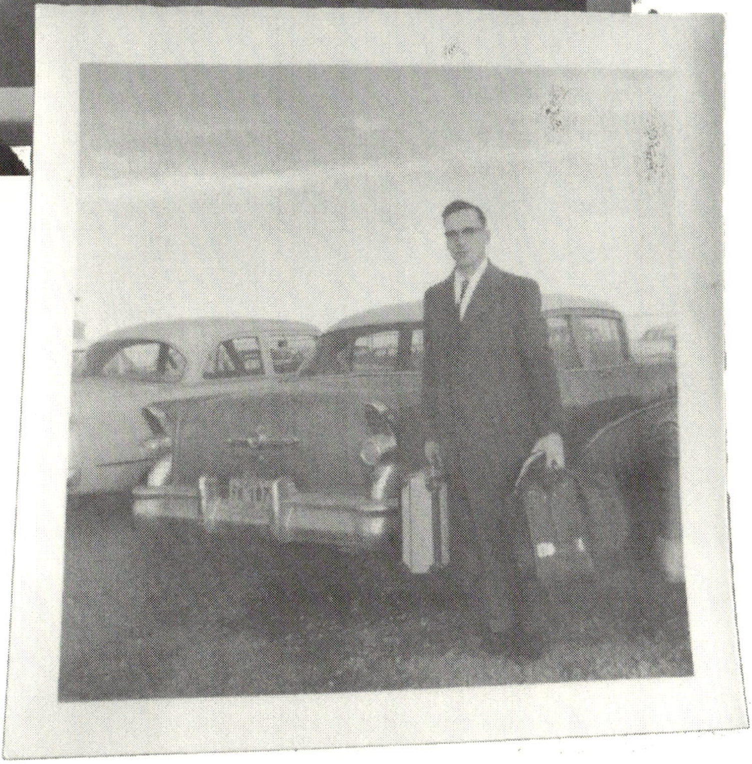

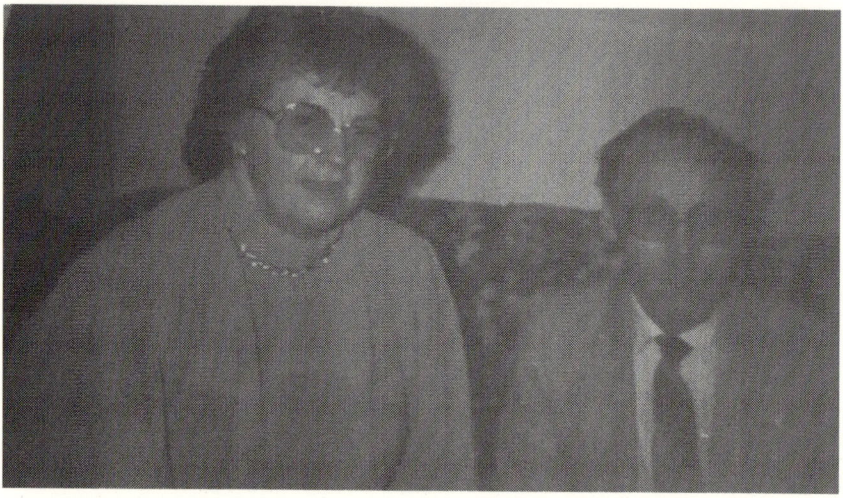

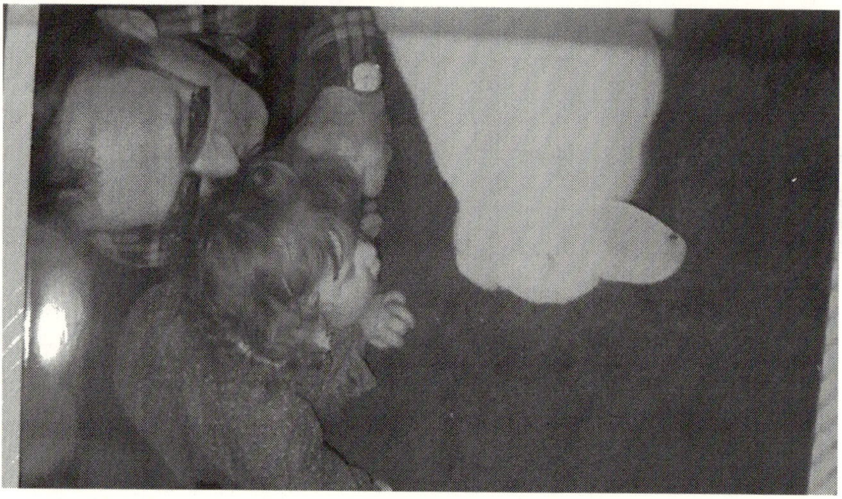

MEMOIRS OF PFN

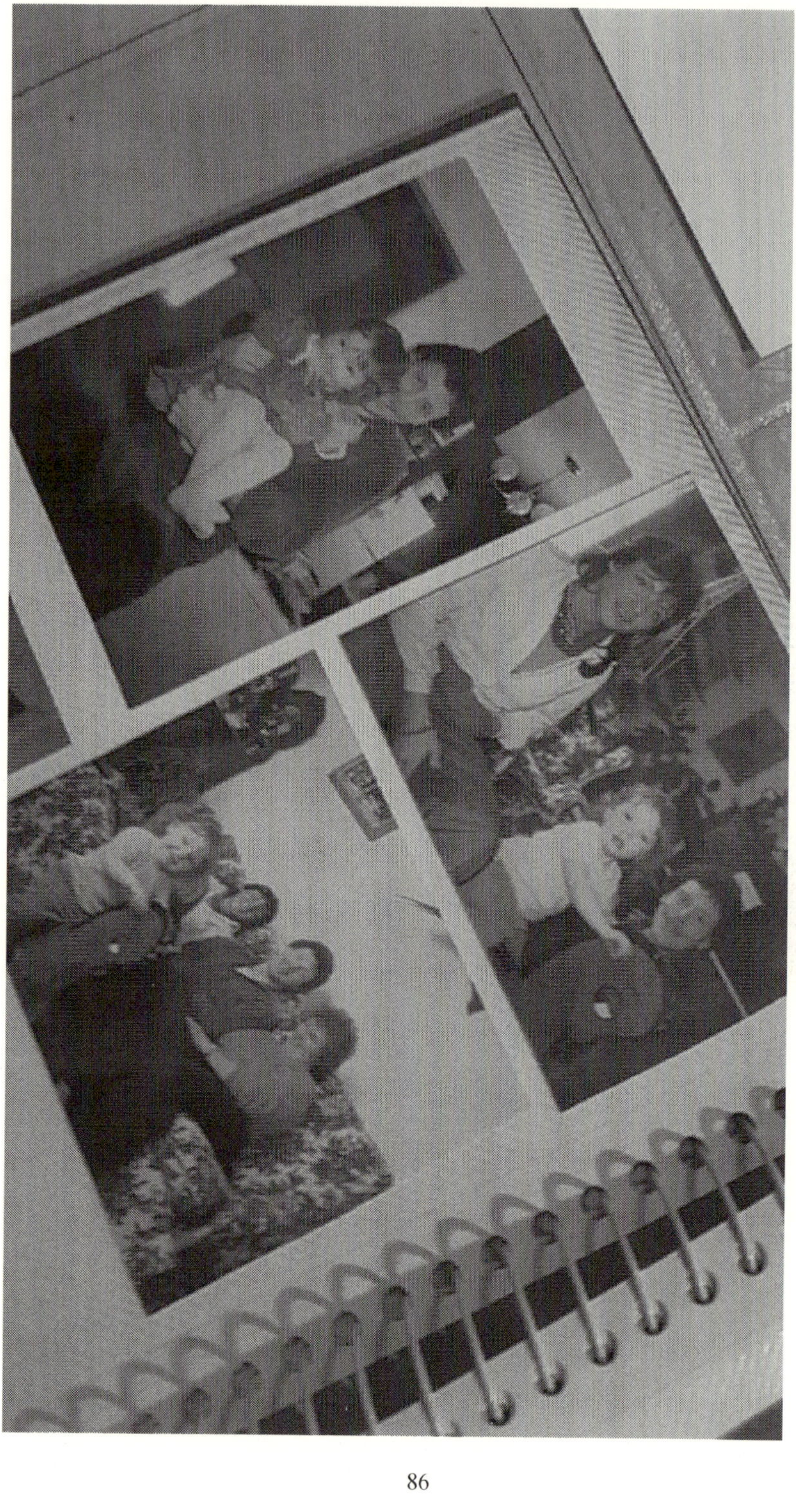

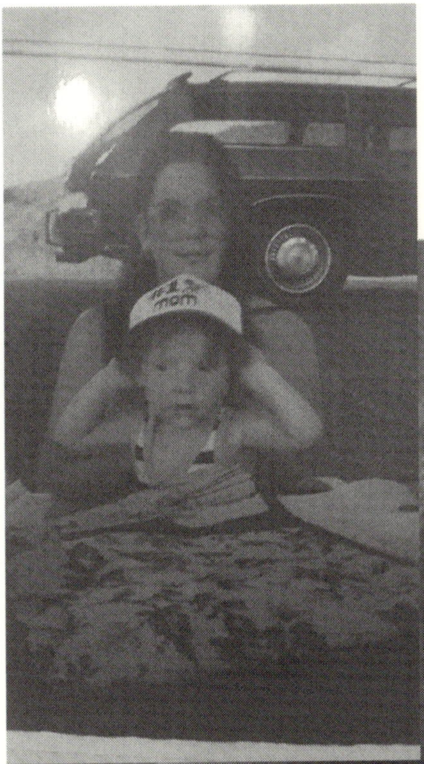
mom

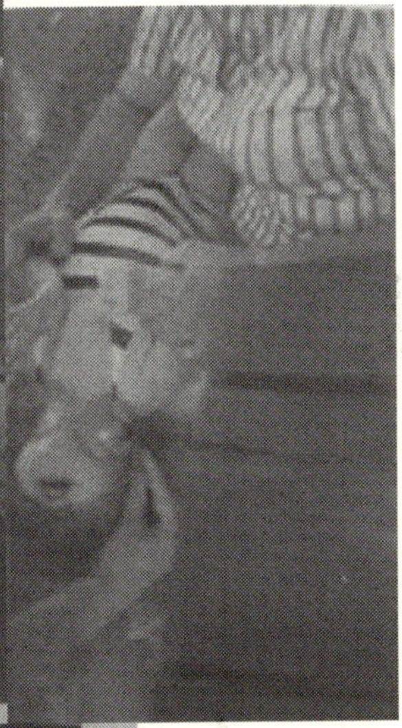

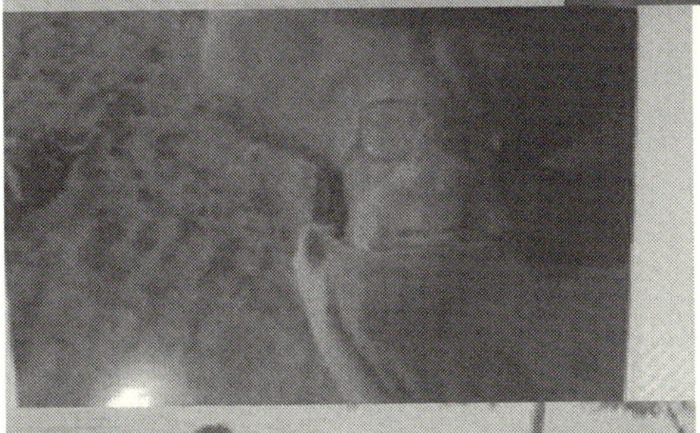

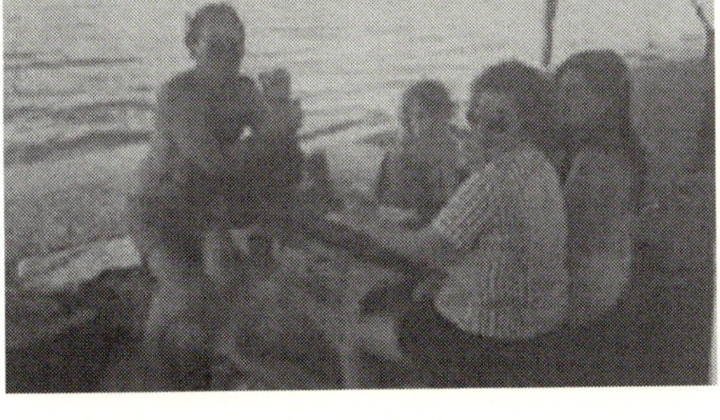

PAUL FERNAND NEDELEC

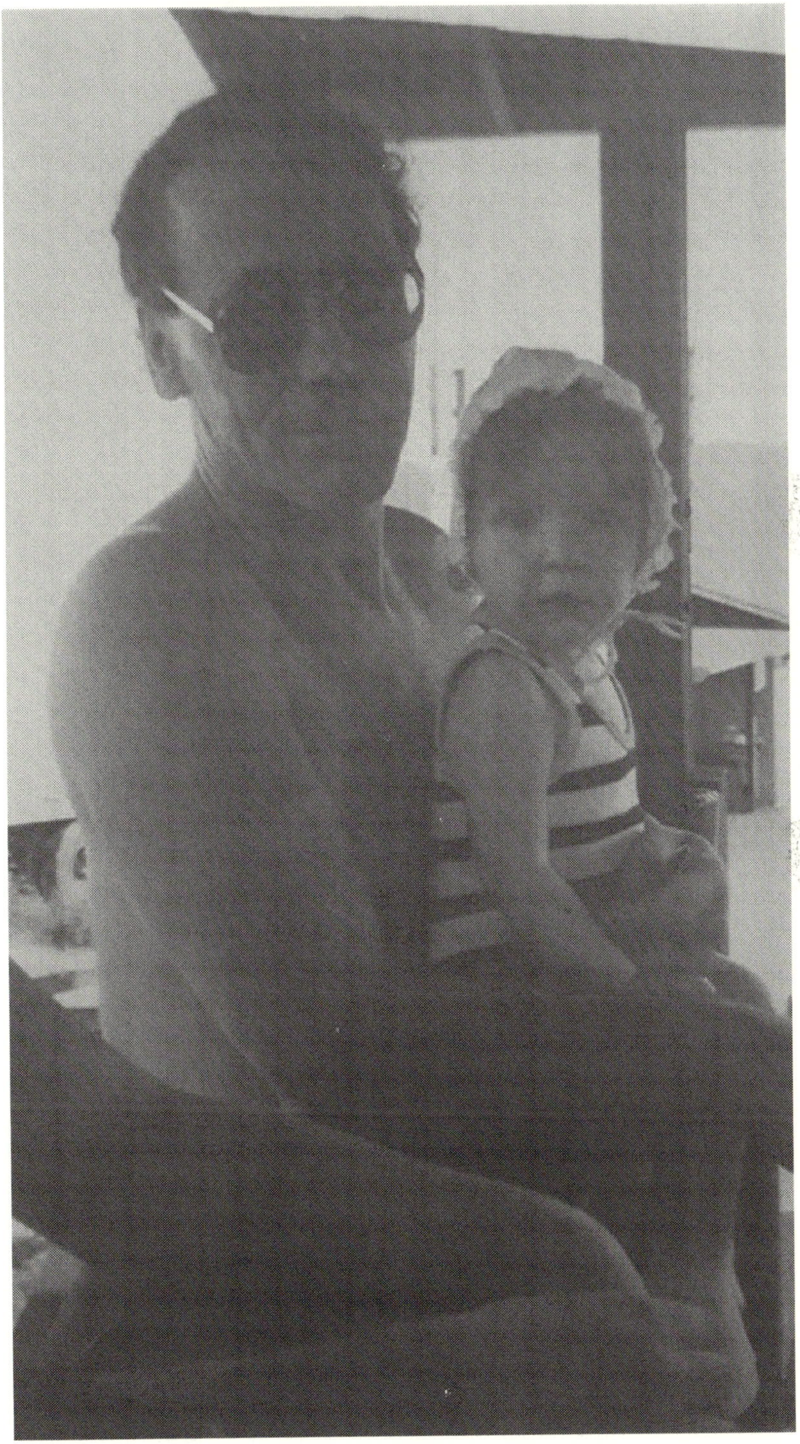

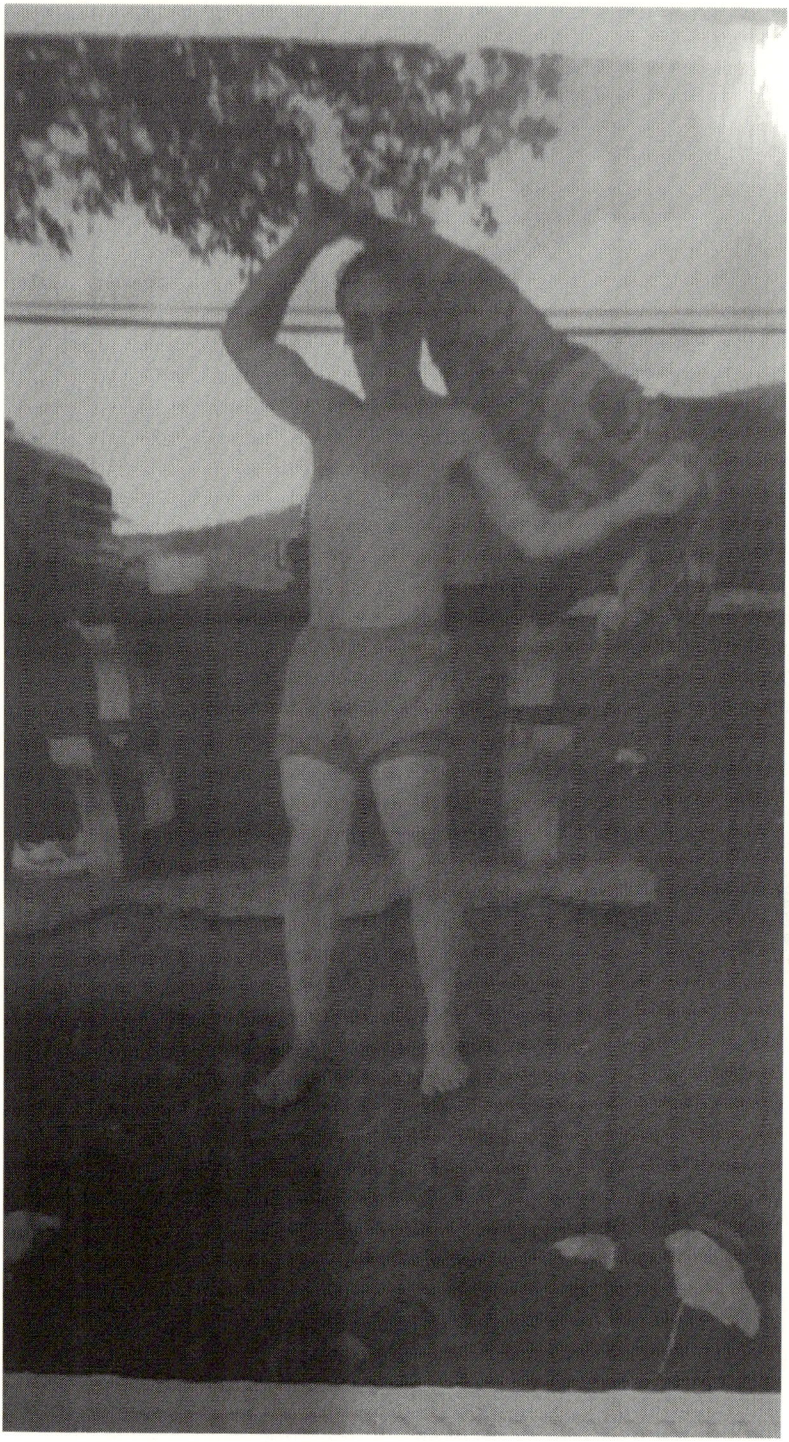

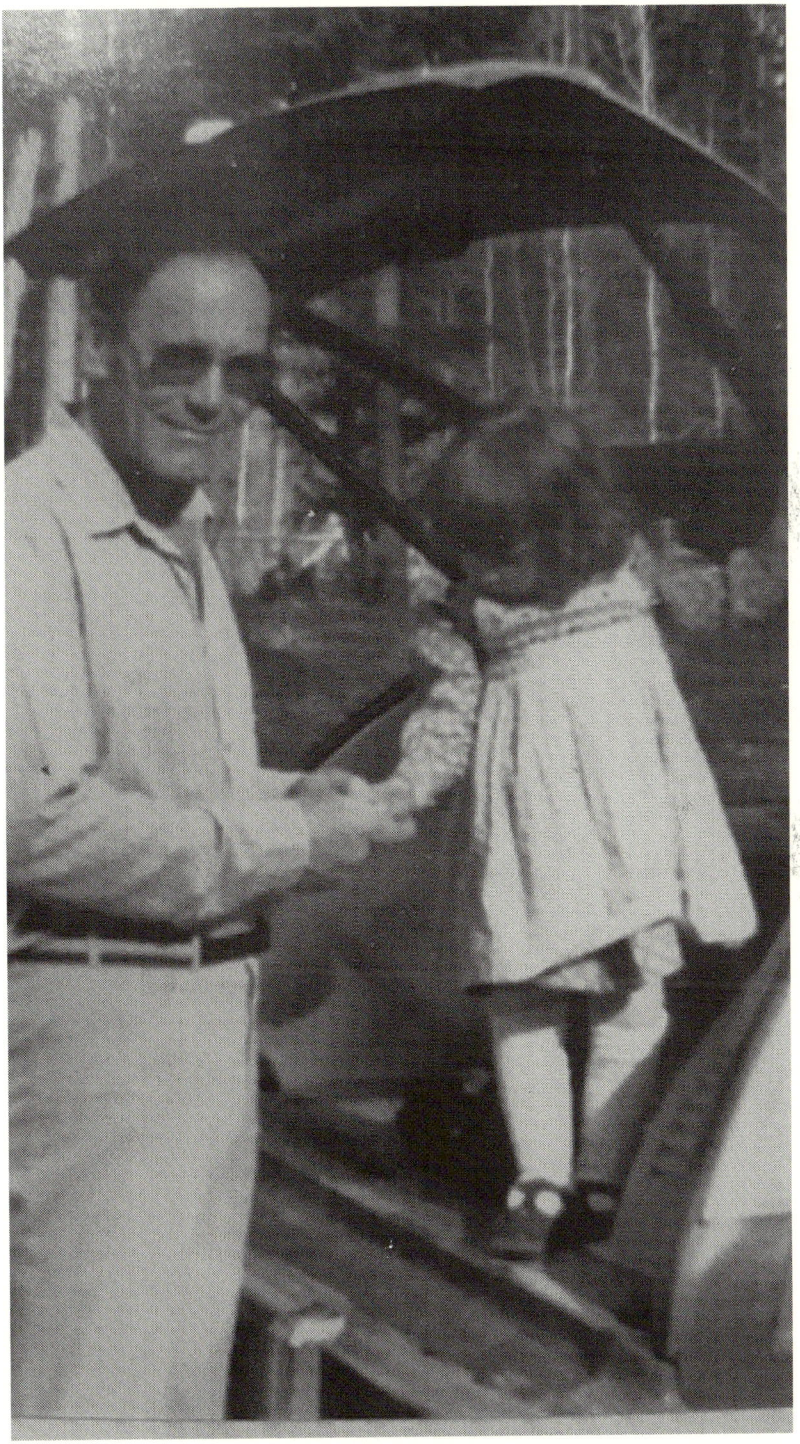

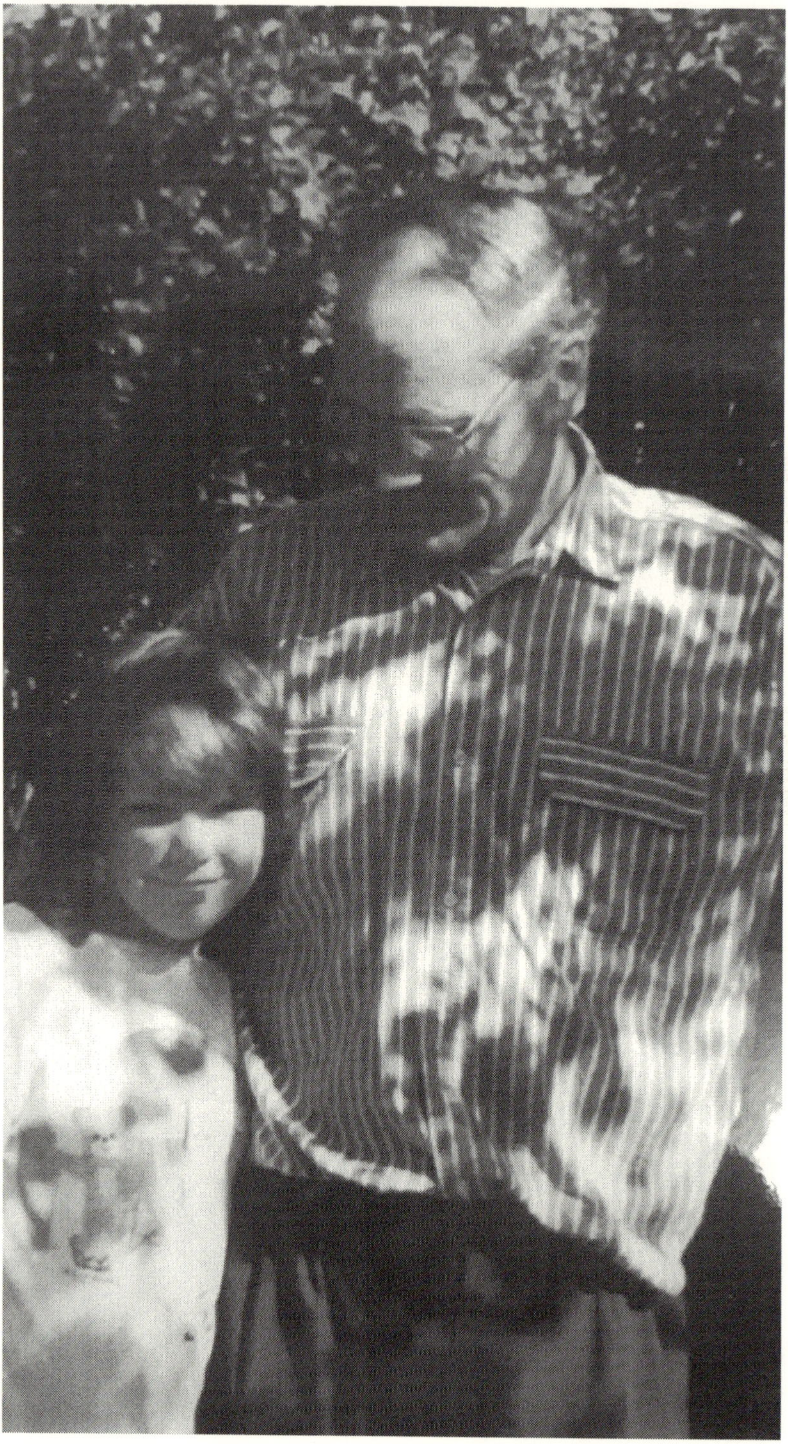

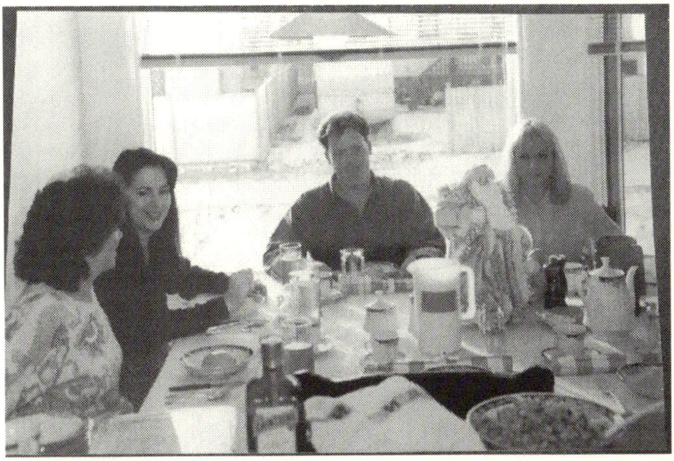

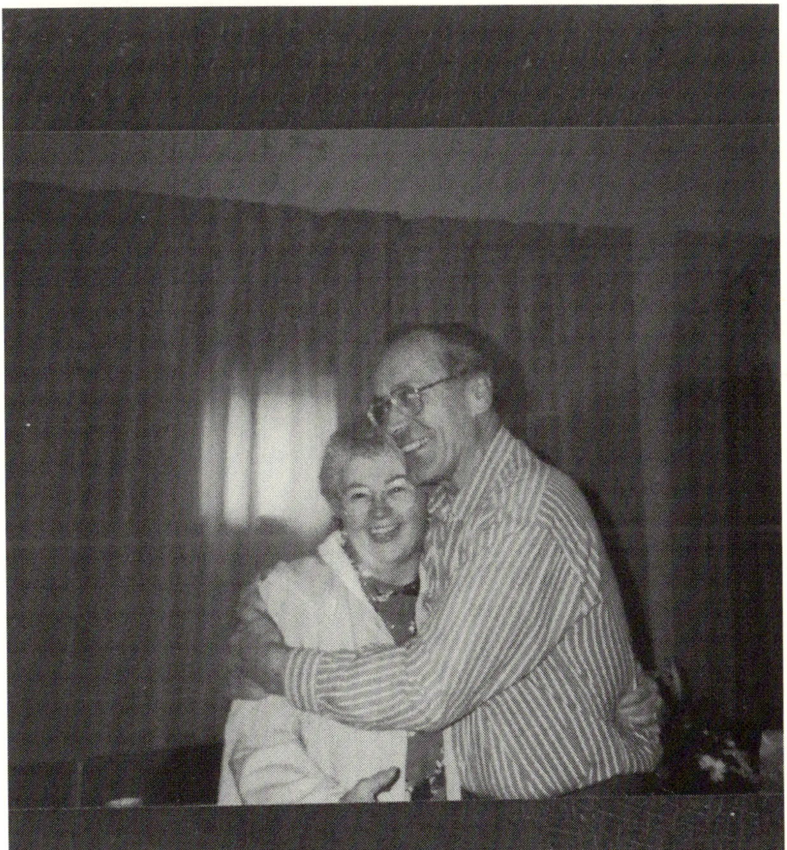

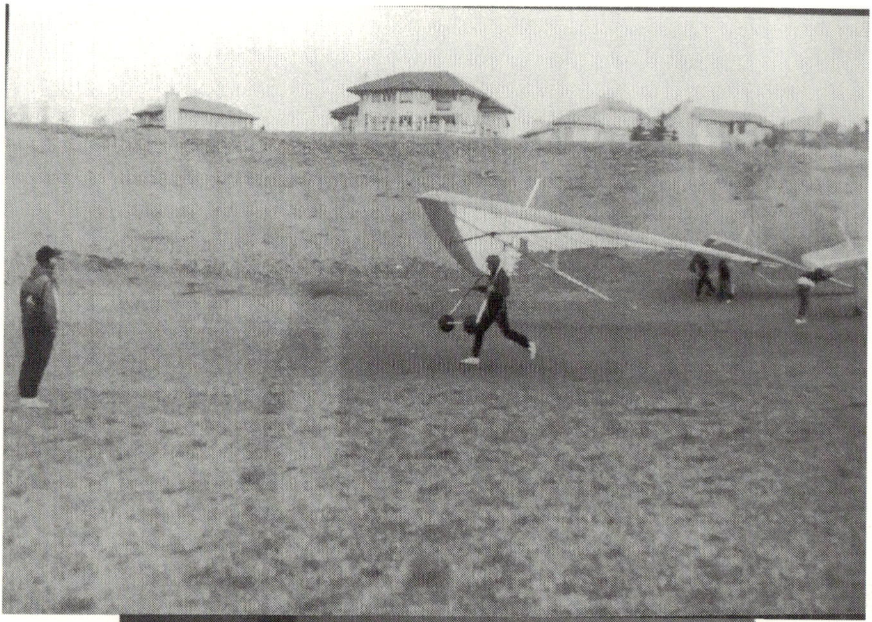

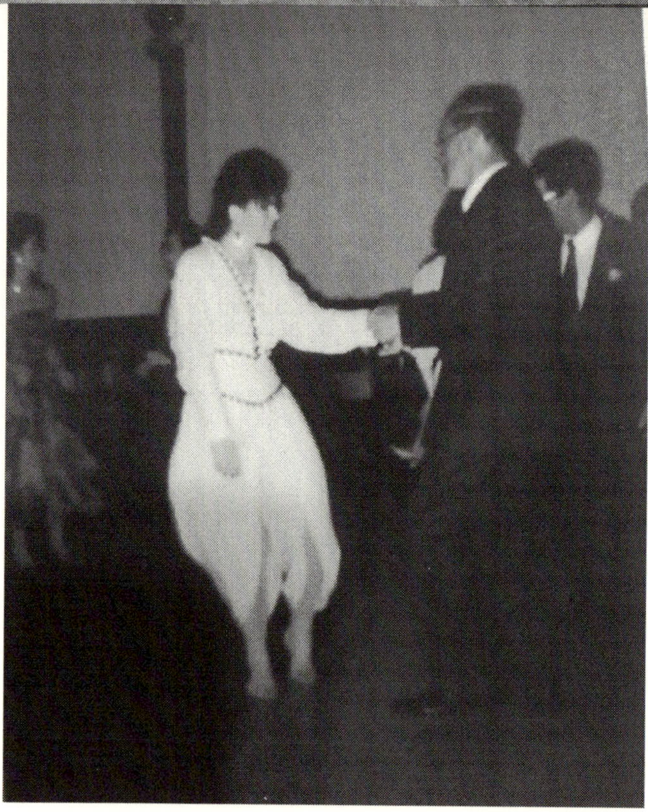

MEMOIRS OF PFN

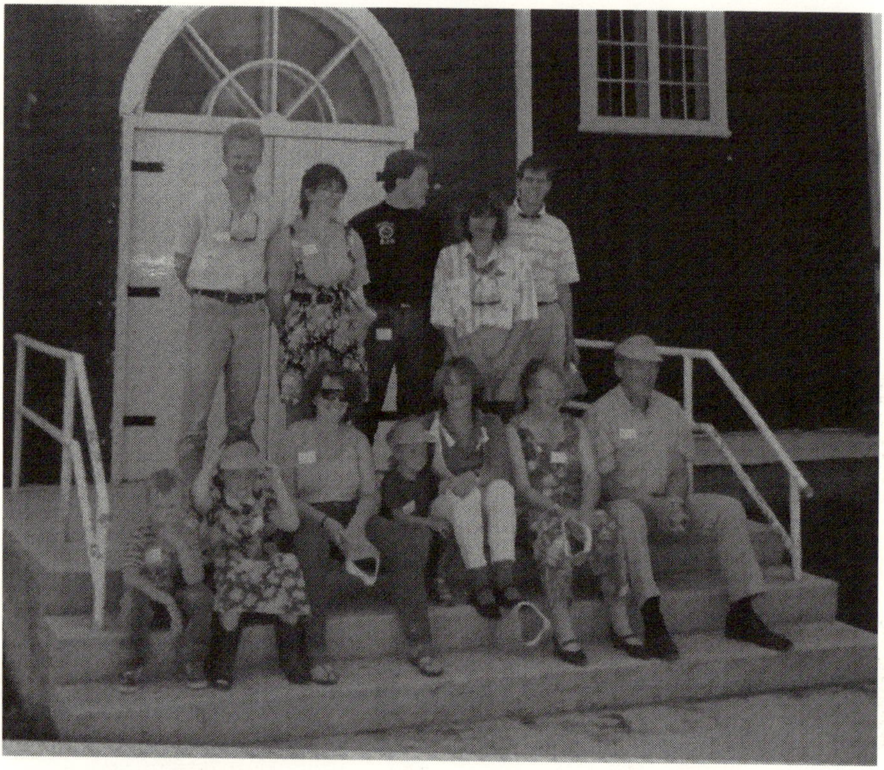

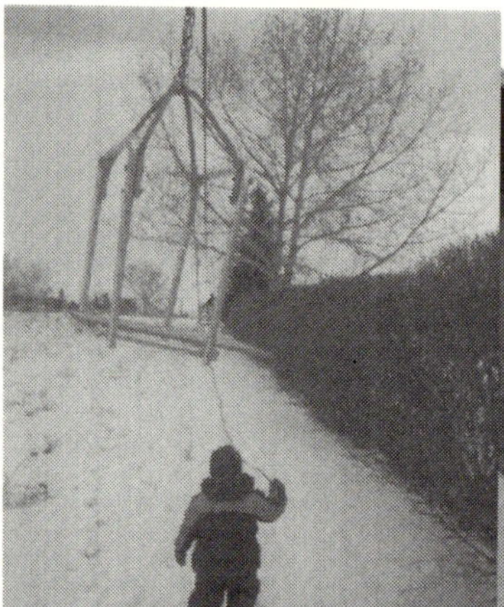

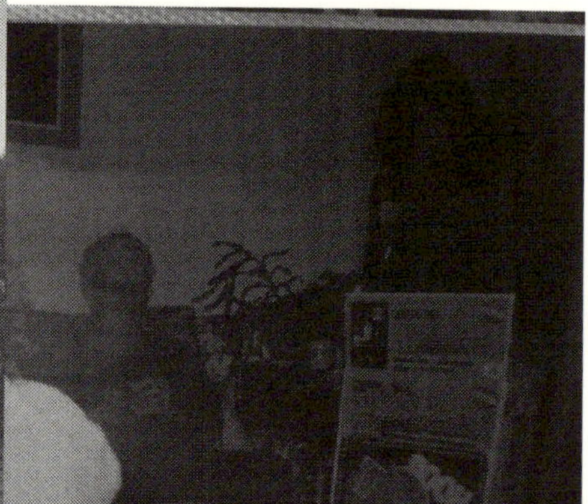

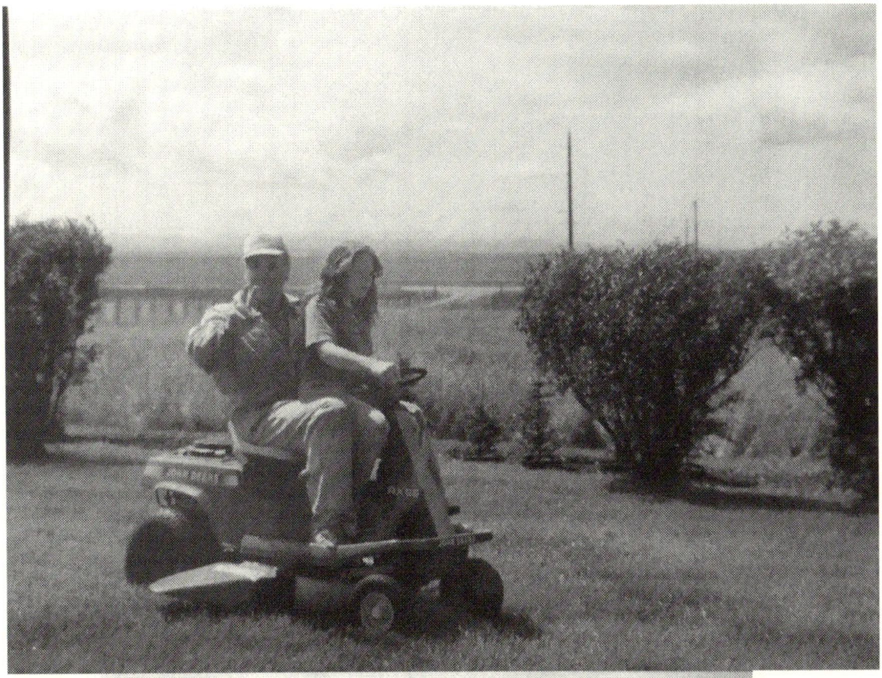

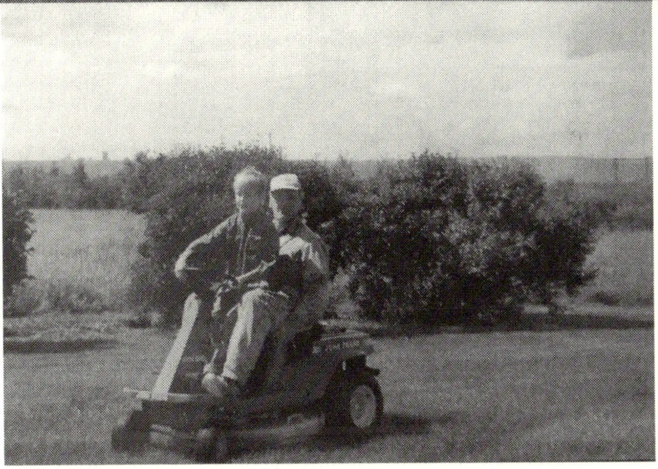

PAUL FERNAND NEDELEC

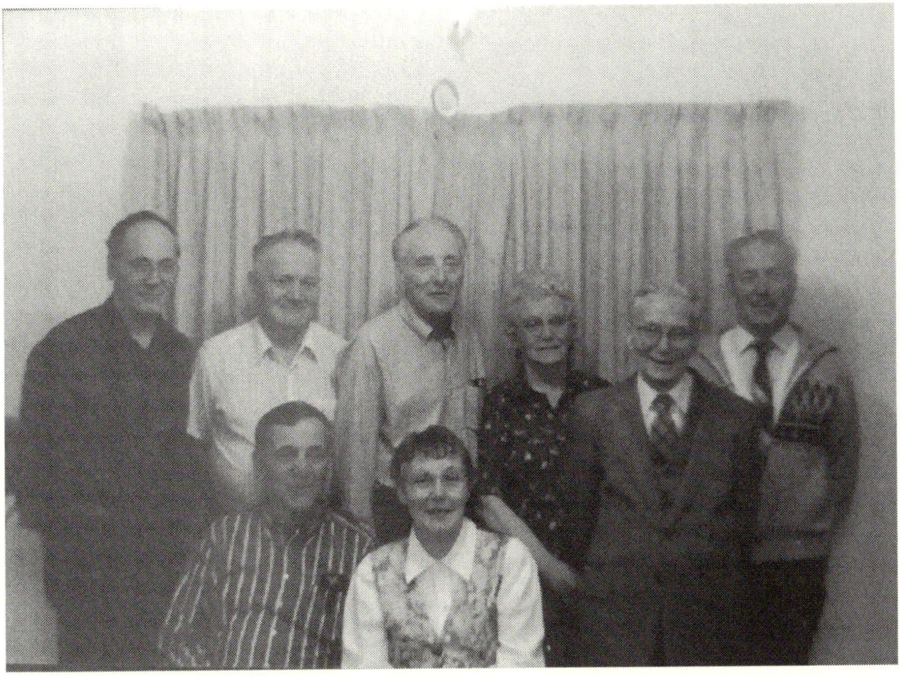

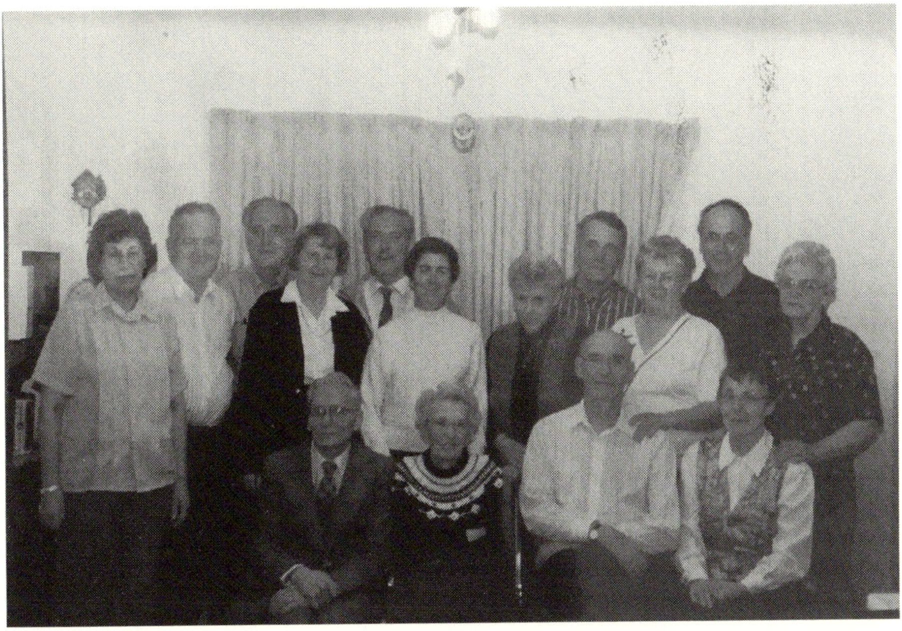

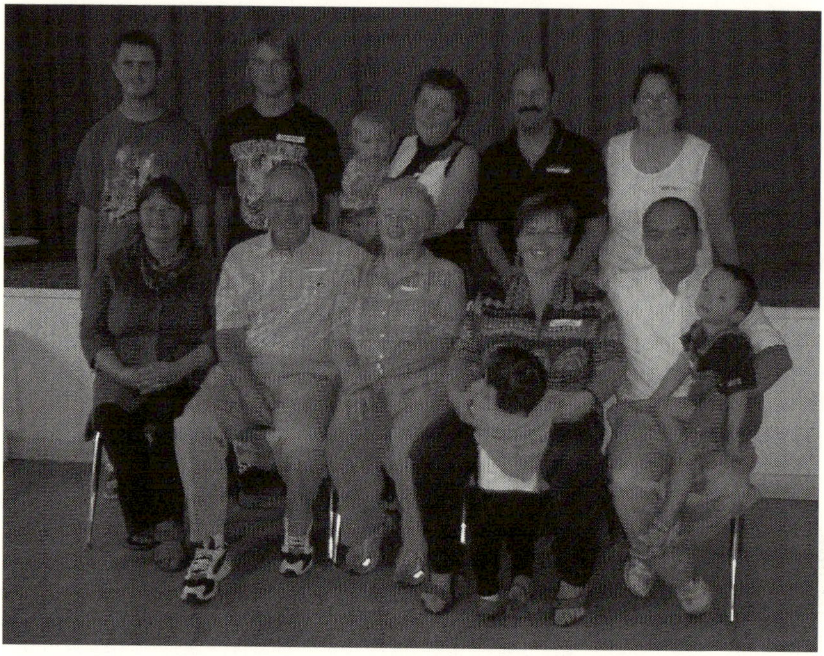

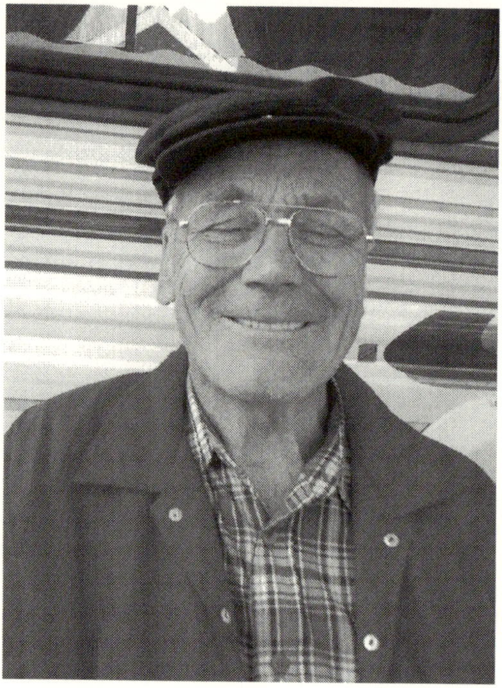

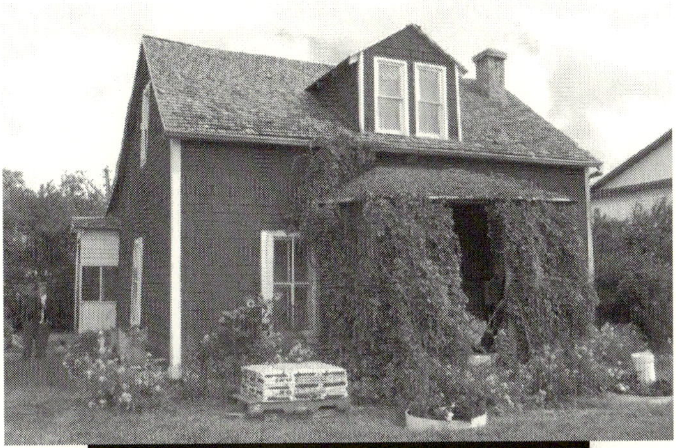

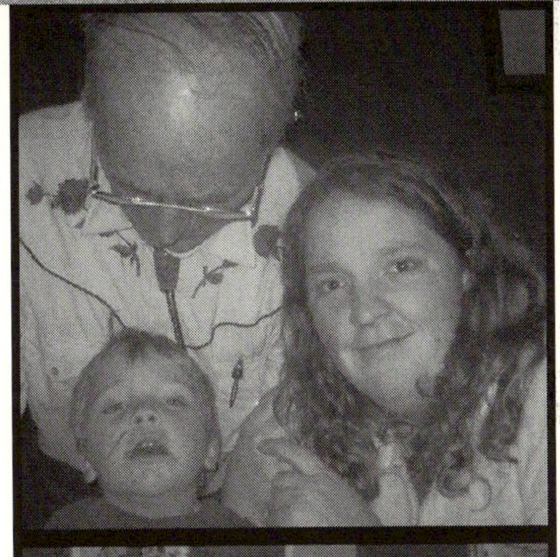

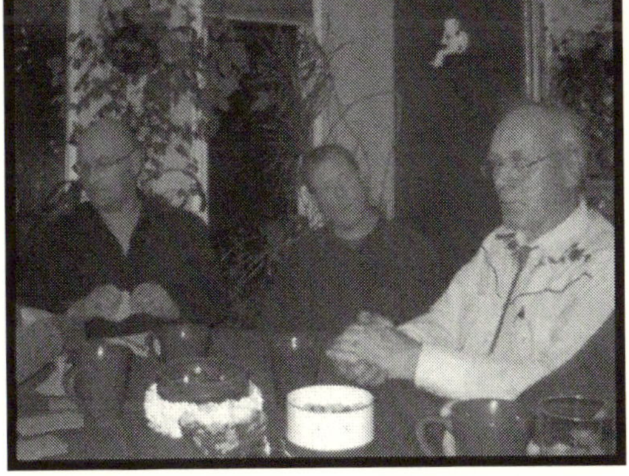

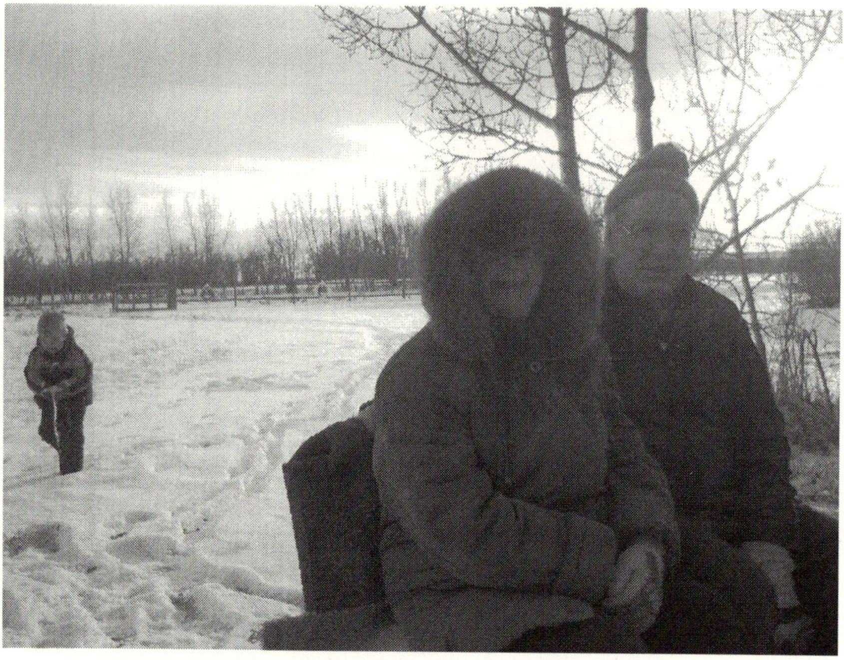

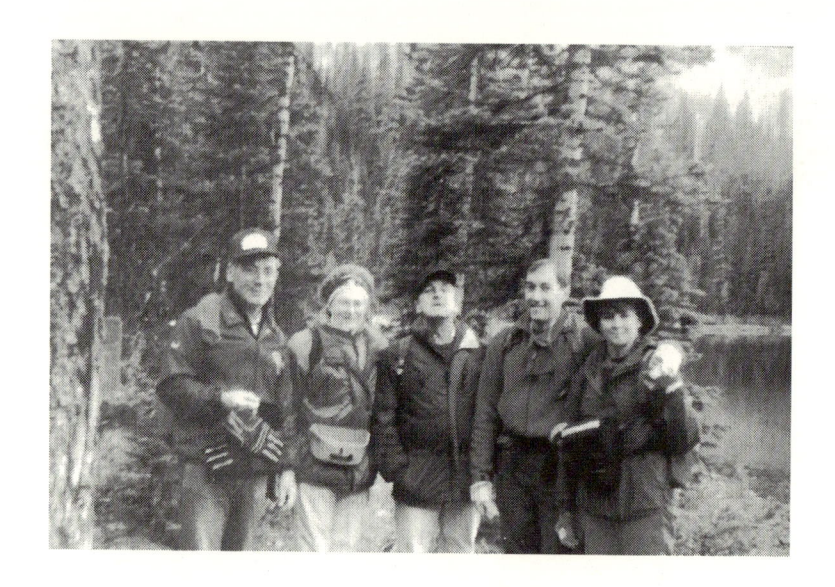

MEMOIRS OF PFN

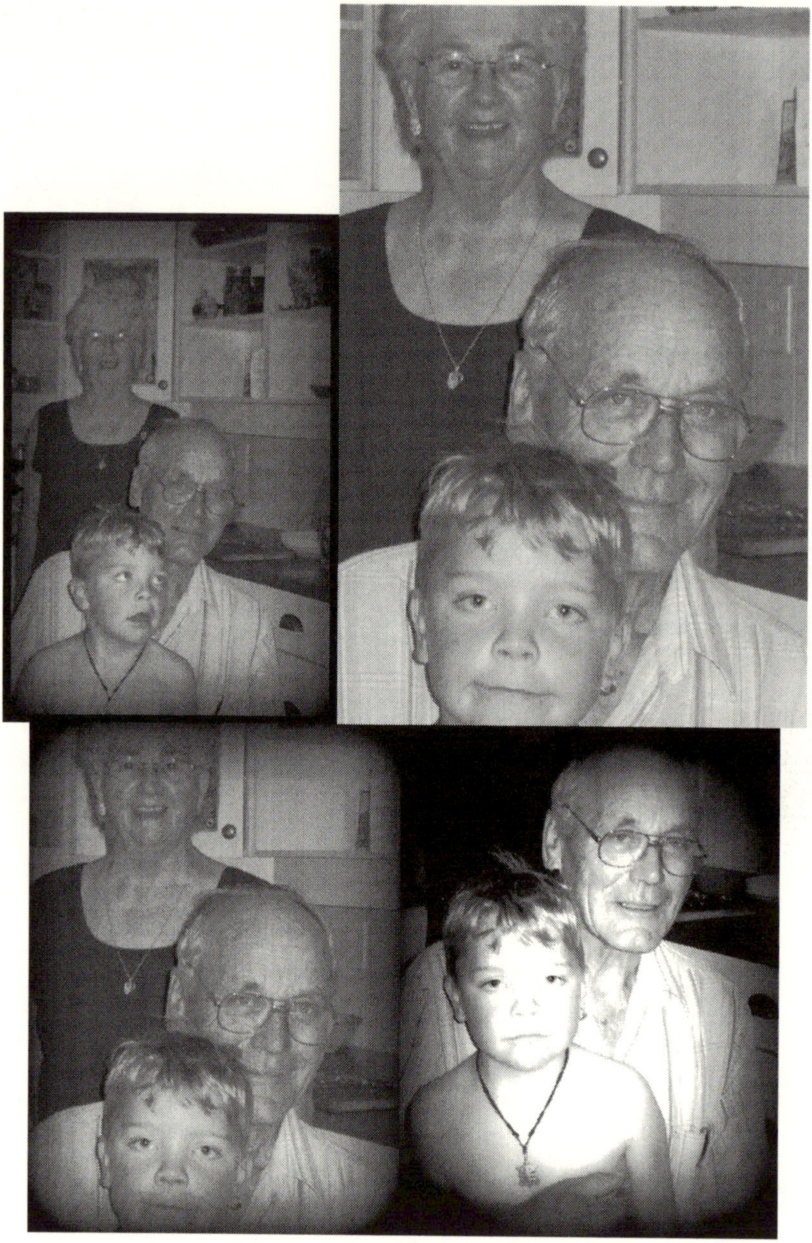

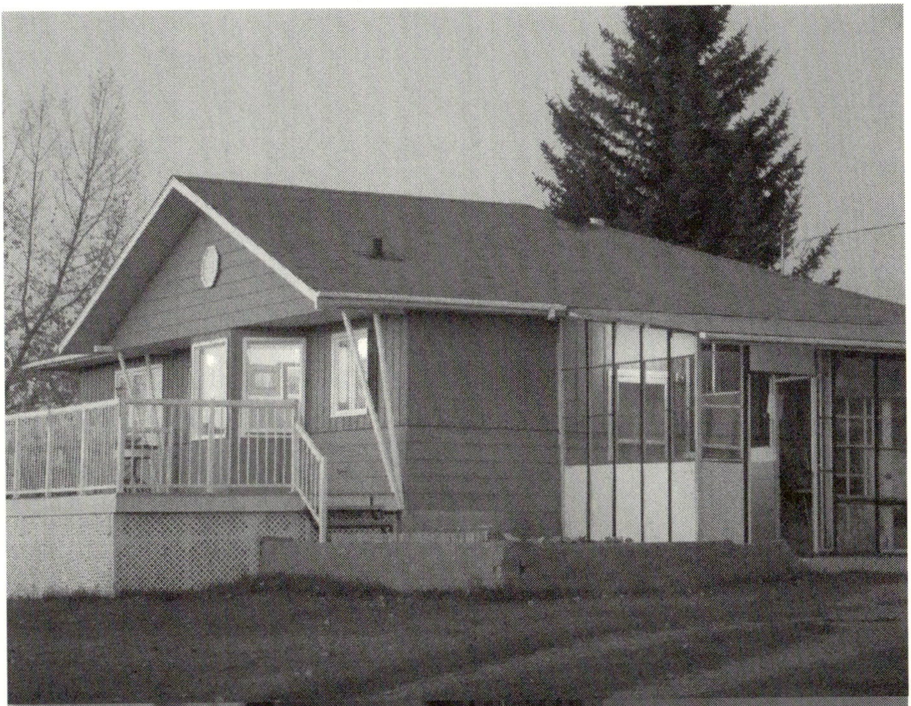

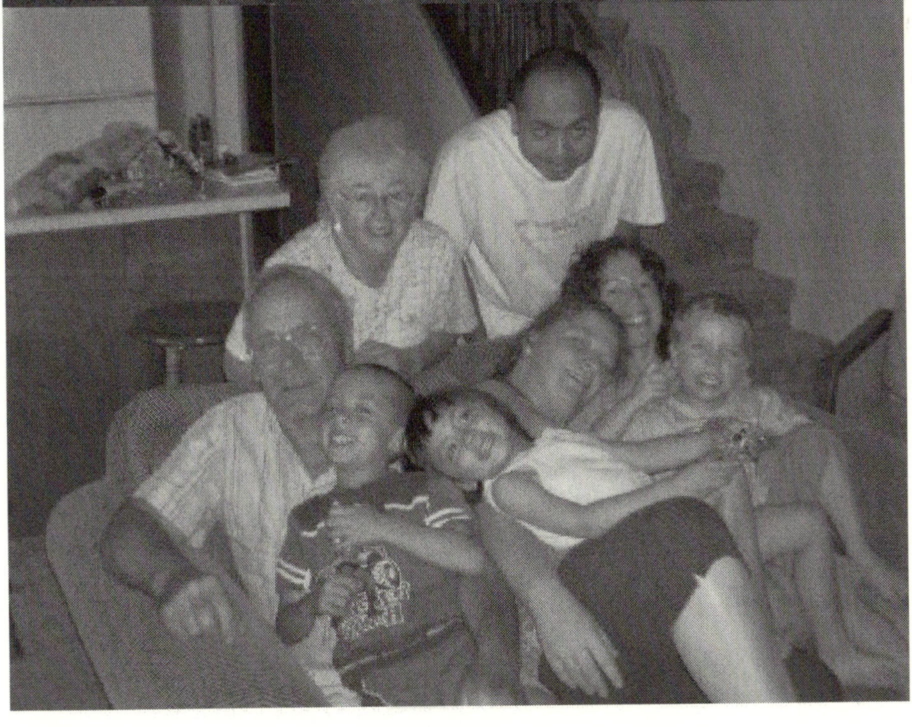

PAUL FERNAND NEDELEC

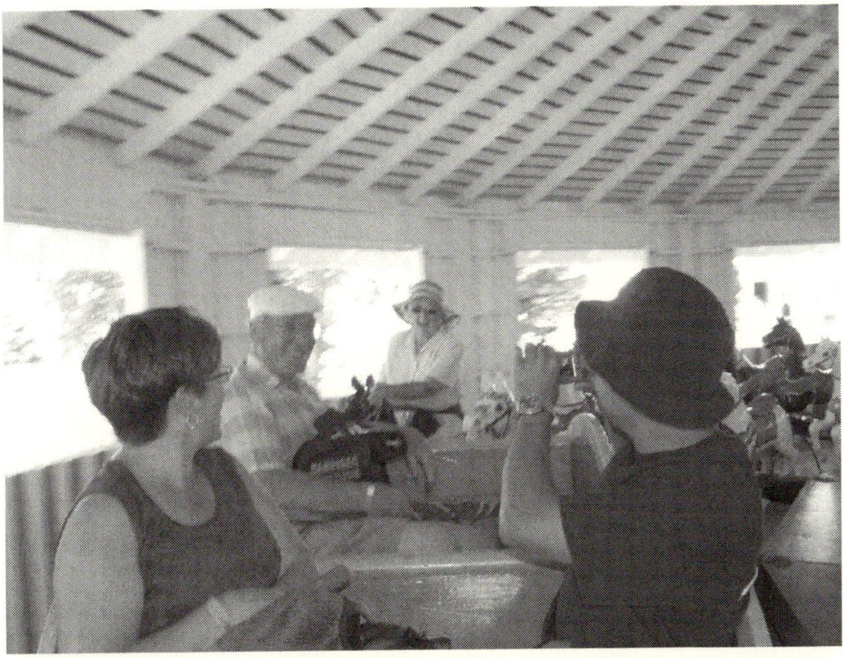

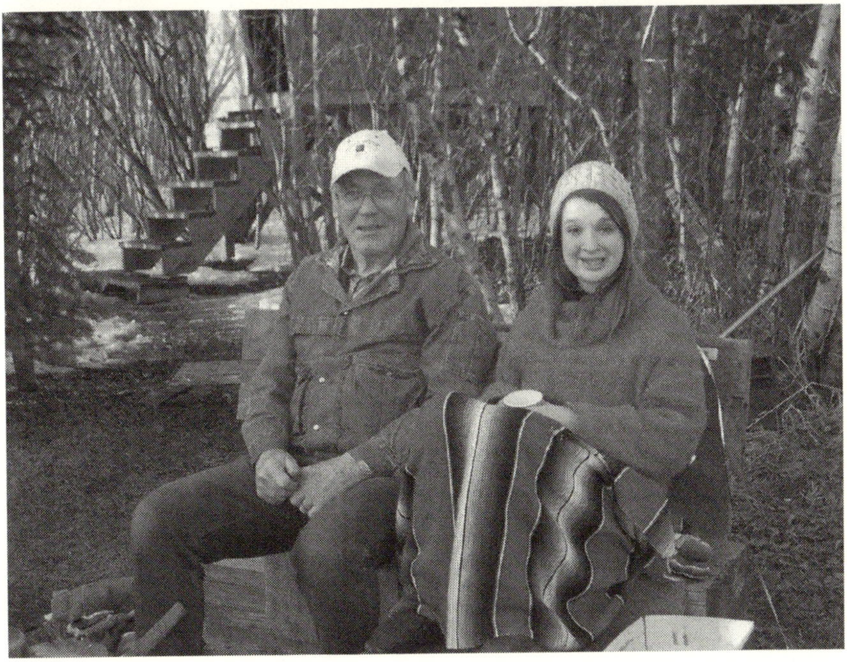

PAUL FERNAND NEDELEC

MEMOIRS OF PFN

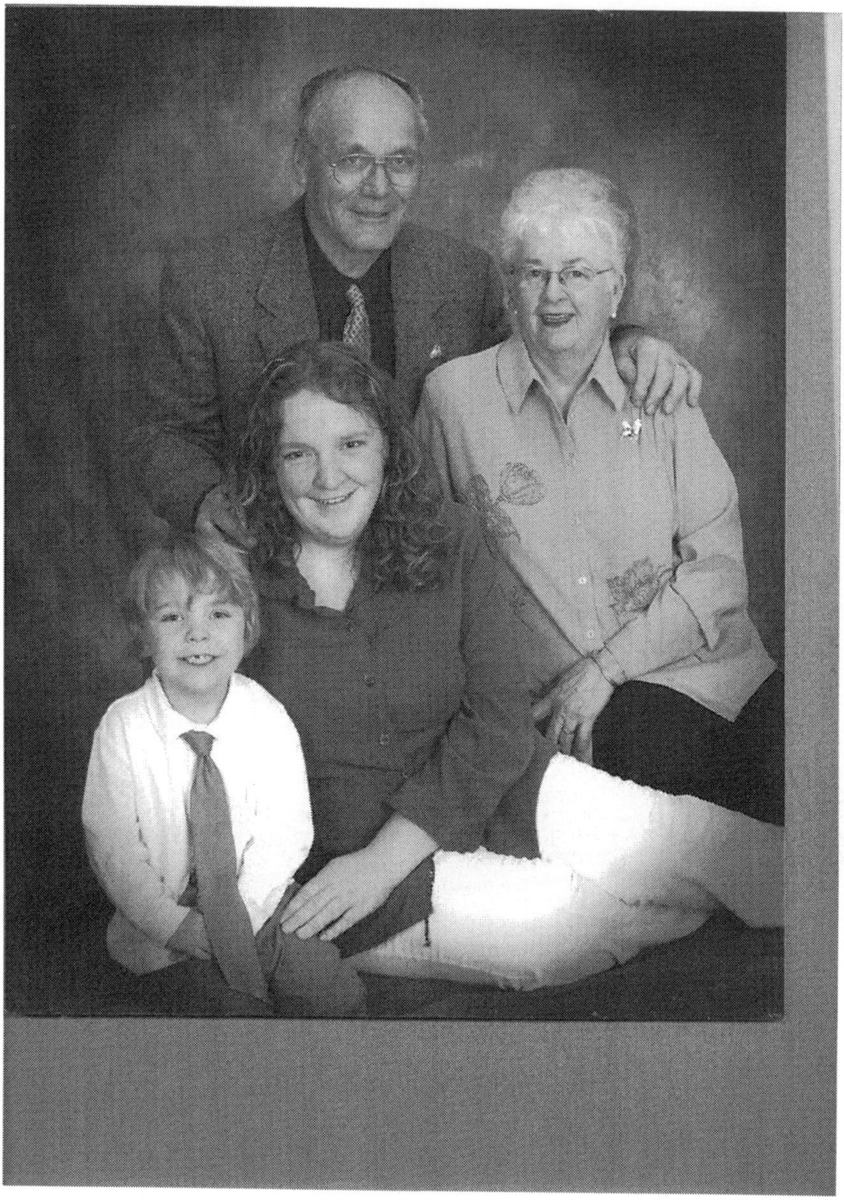

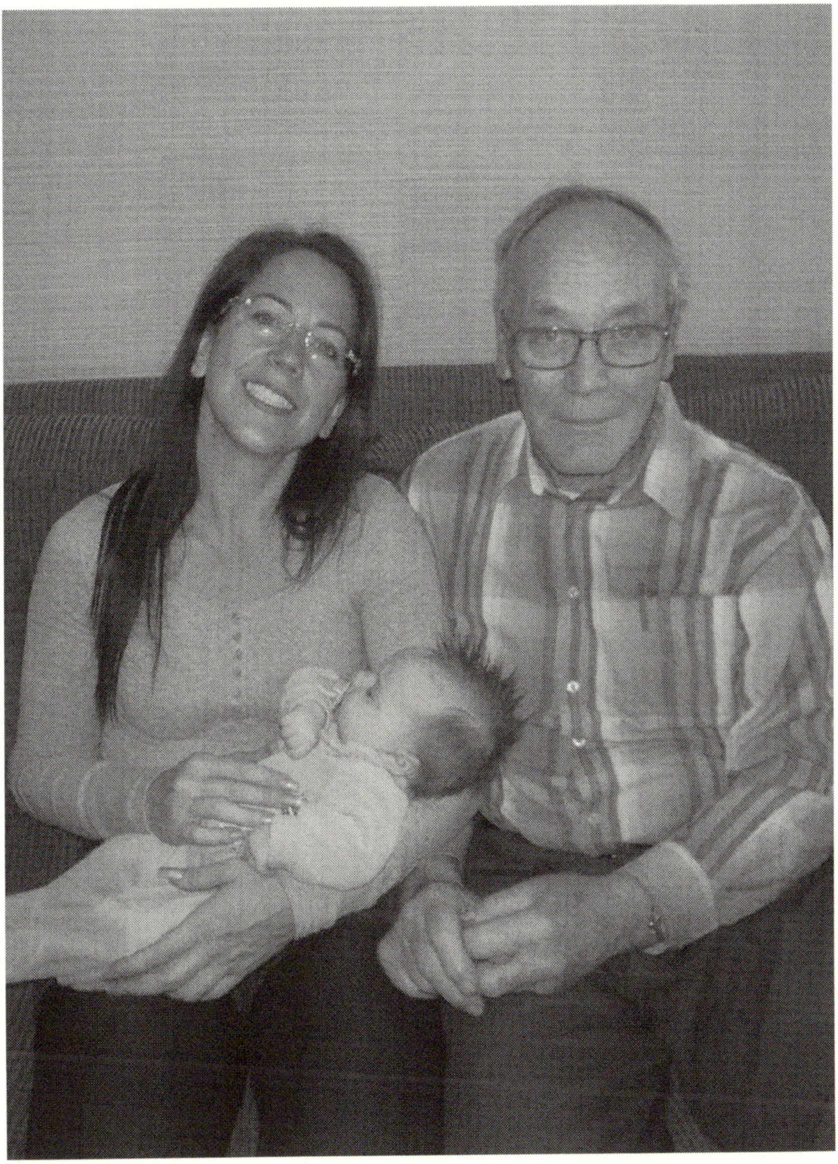

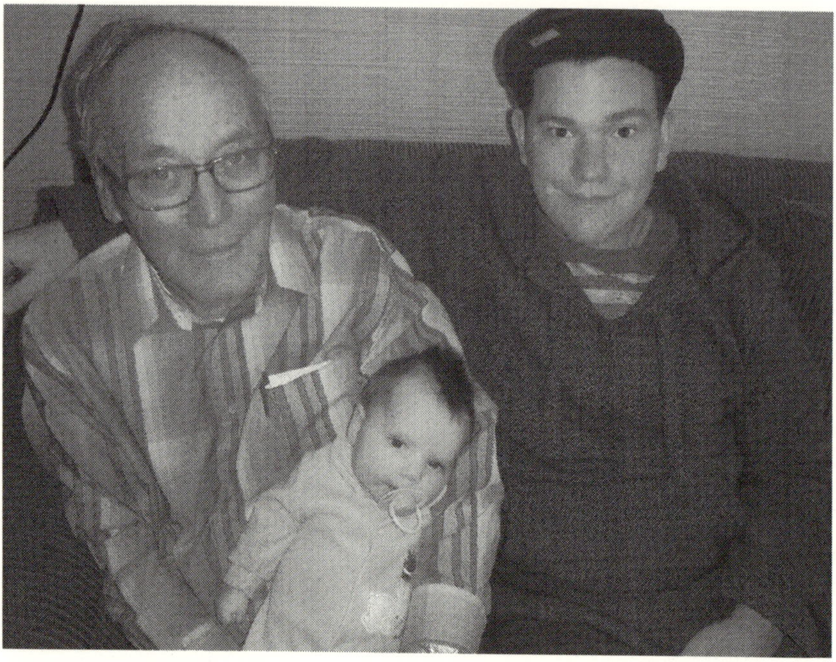

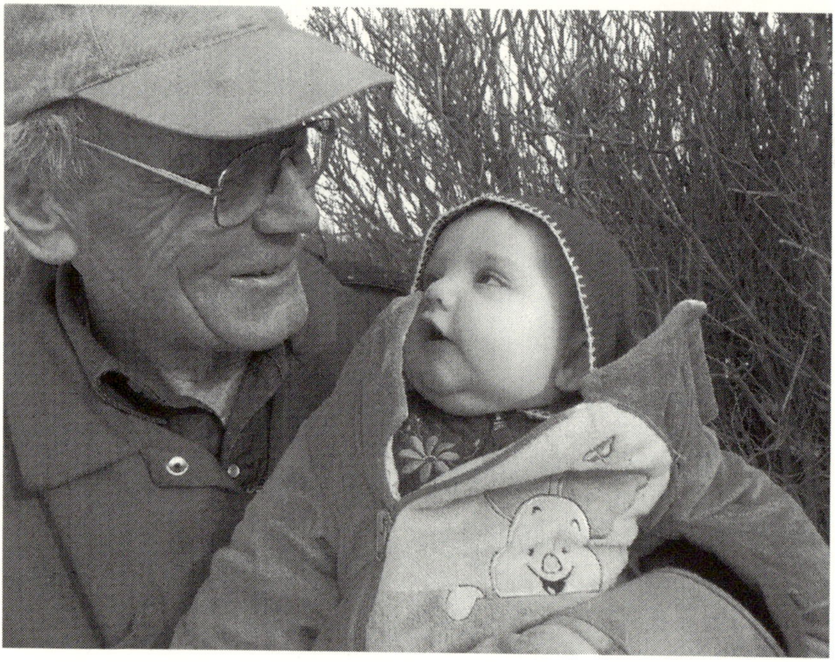

MEMOIRS OF PFN

PAUL FERNAND NEDELEC

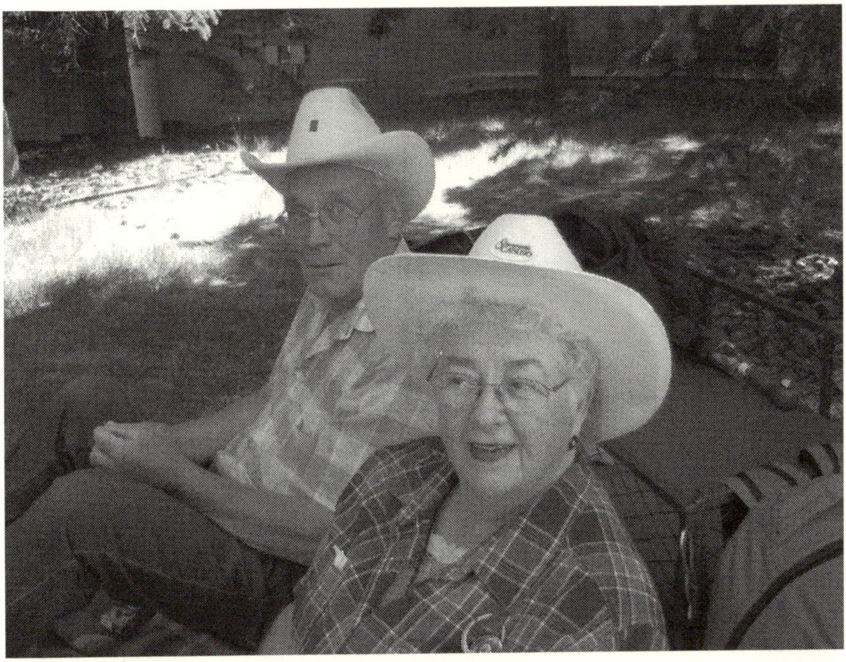

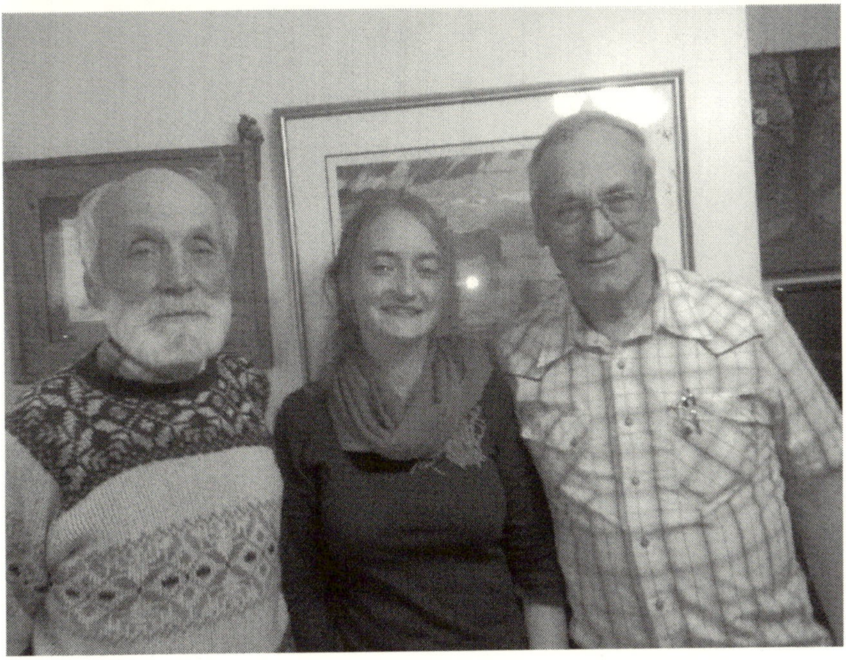

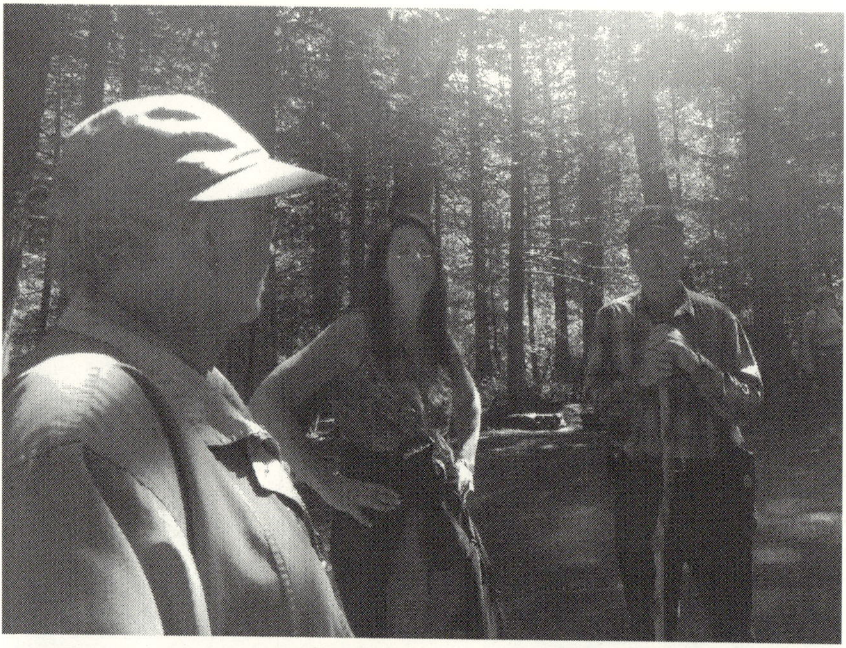

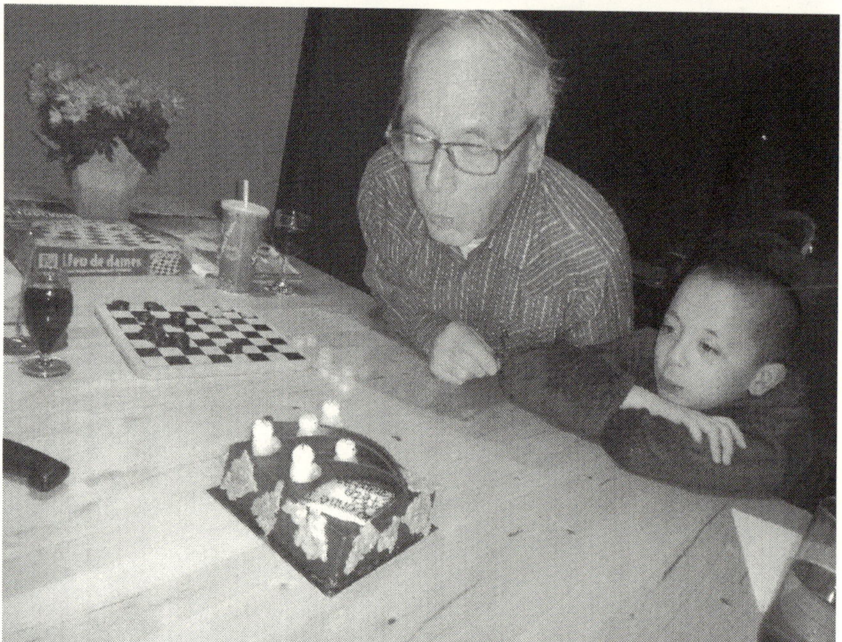

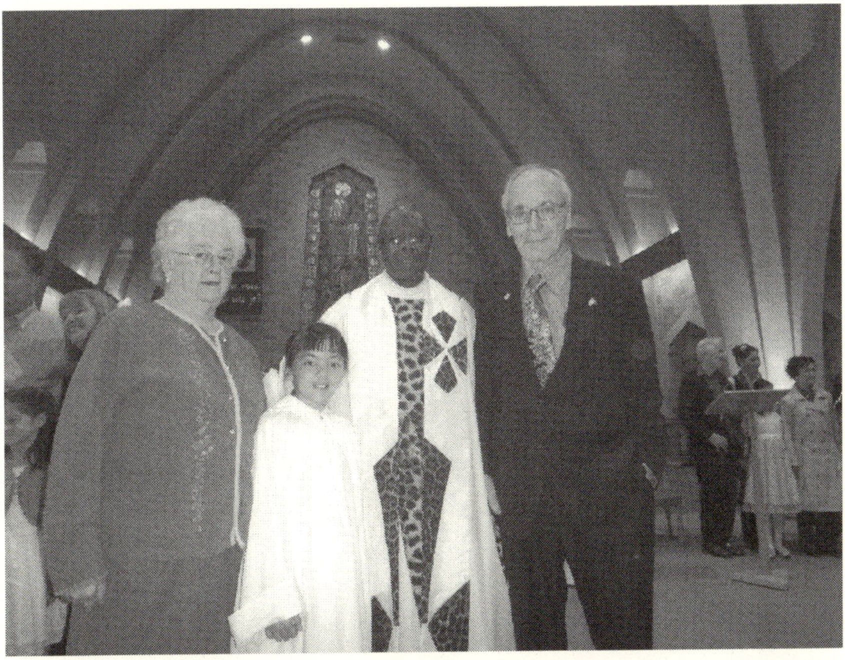

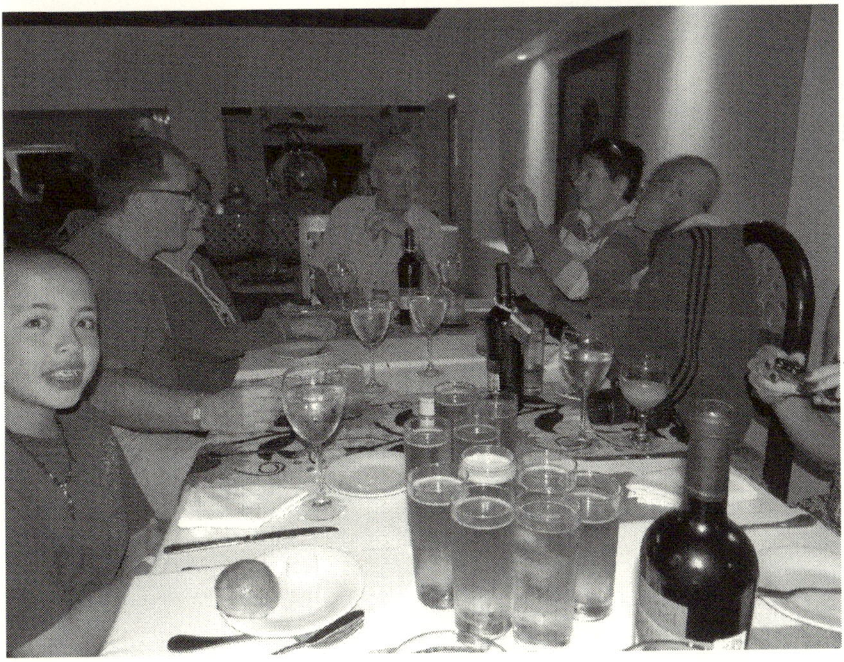

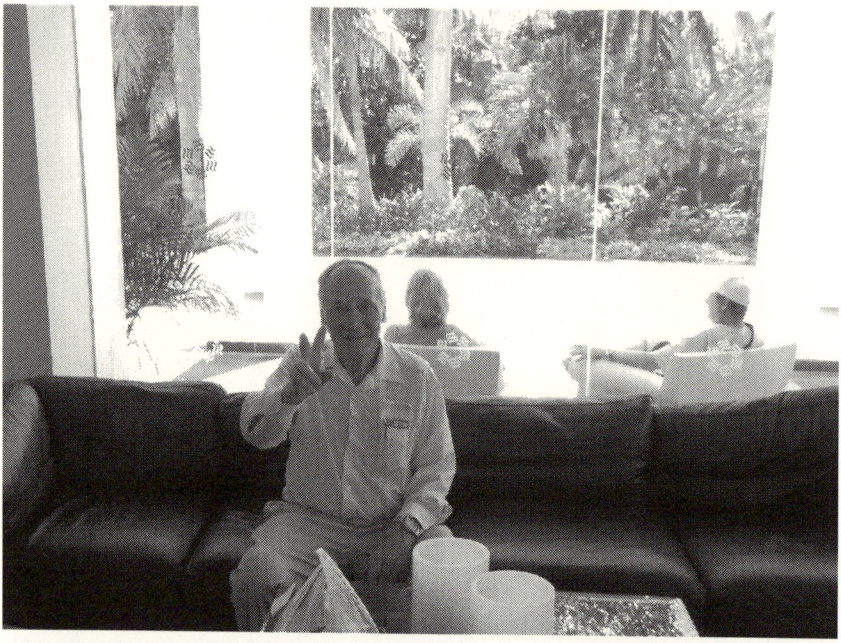

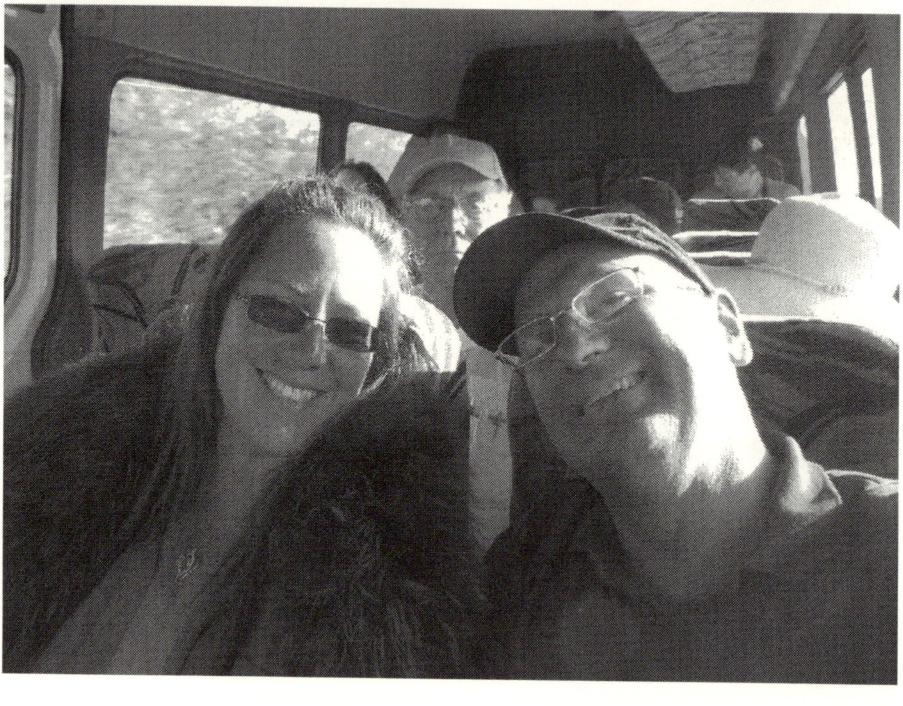

MEMOIRS OF PFN

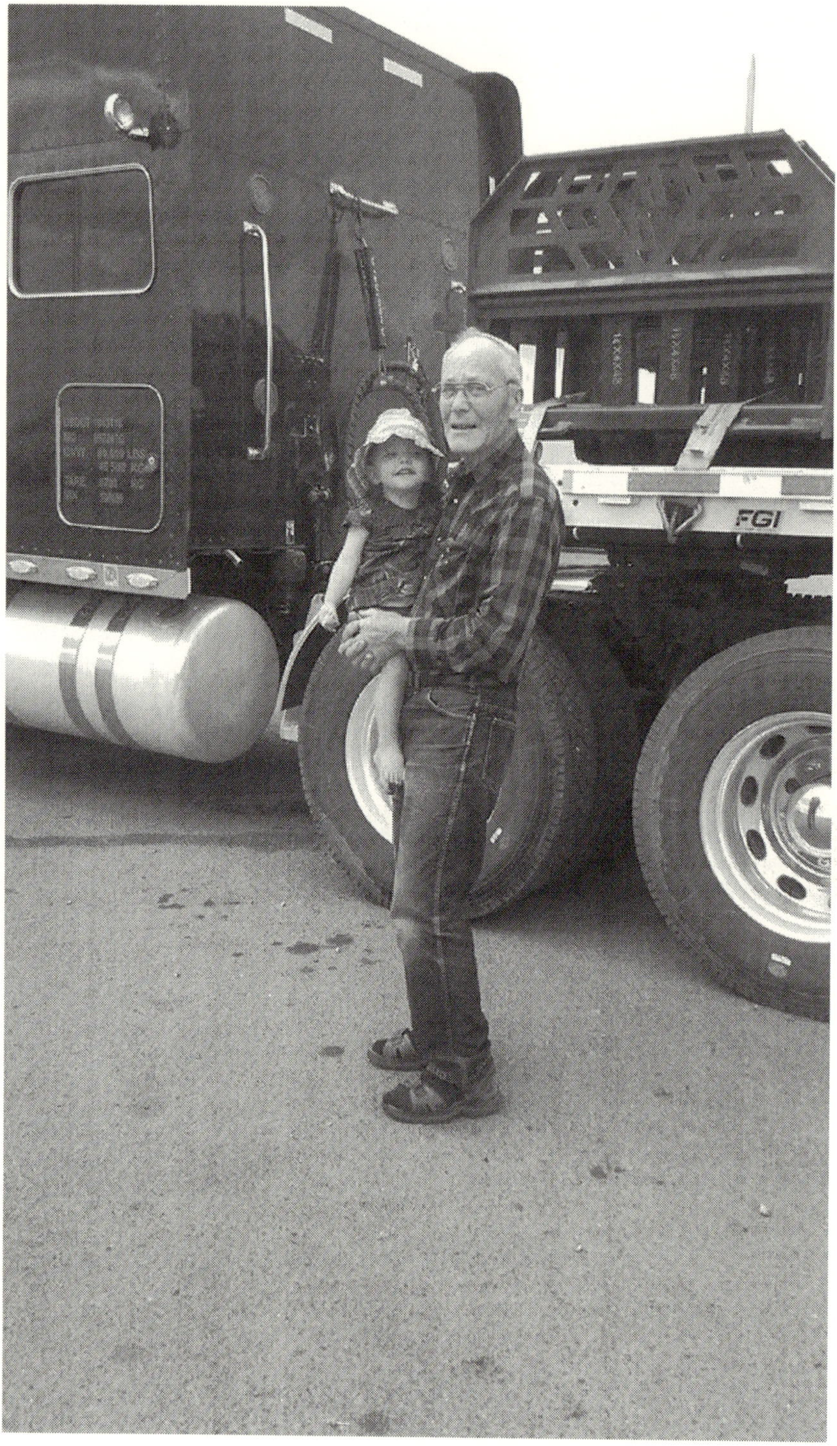
FGI

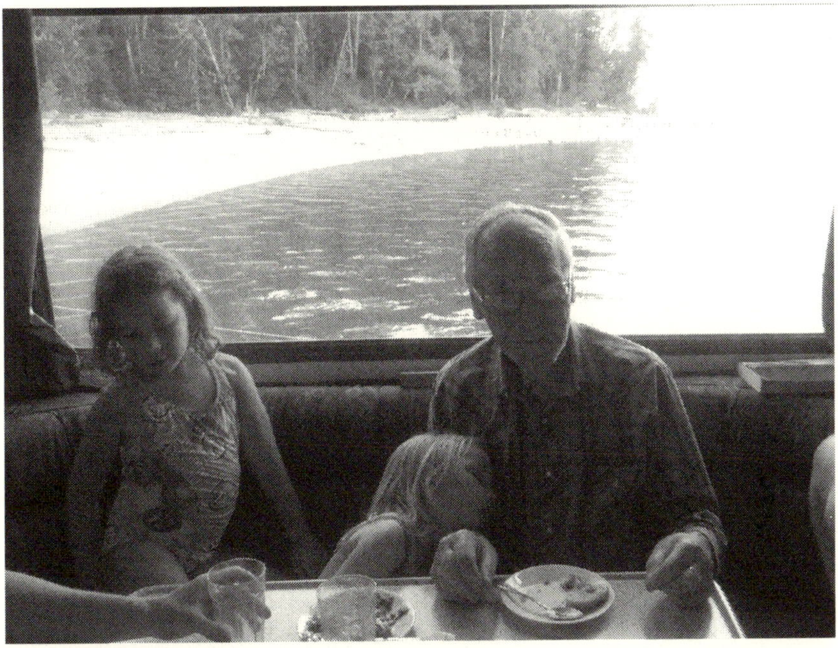

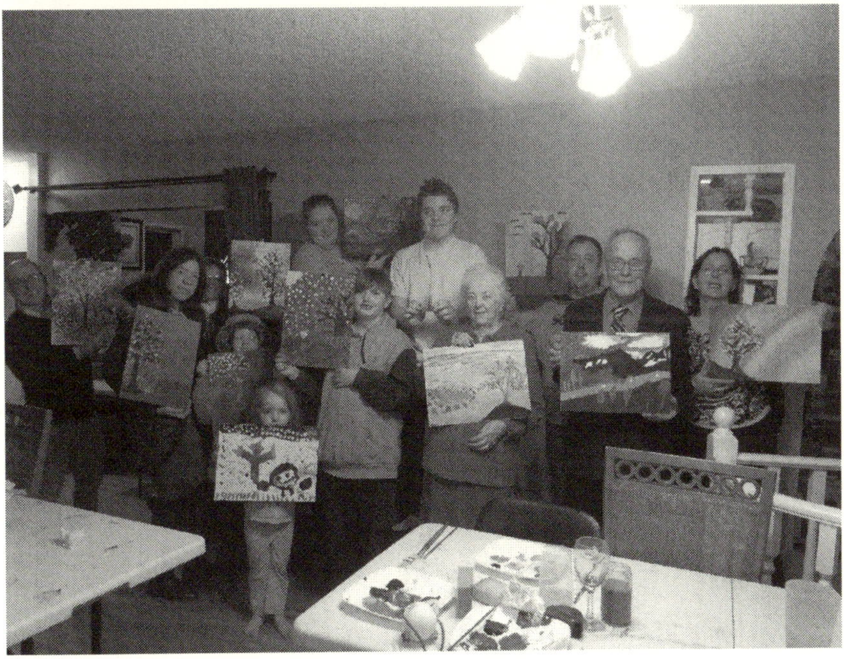

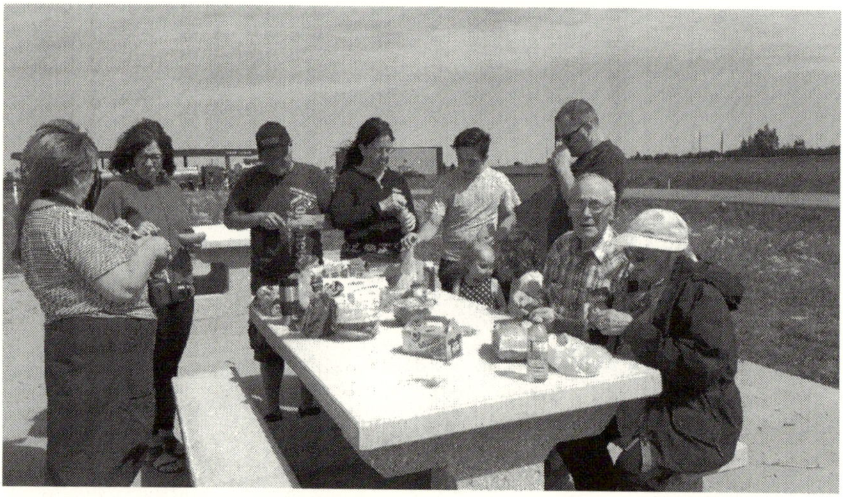

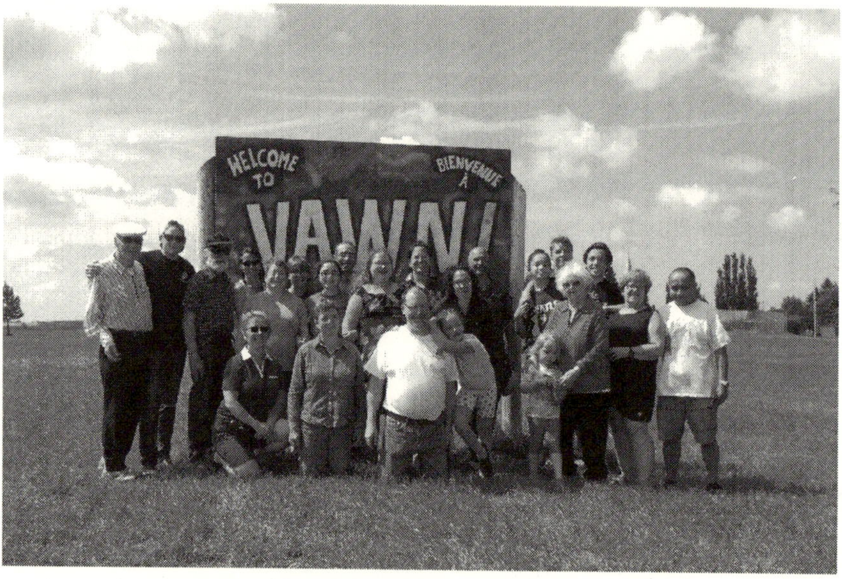
WELCOME TO
BIENVENUE À

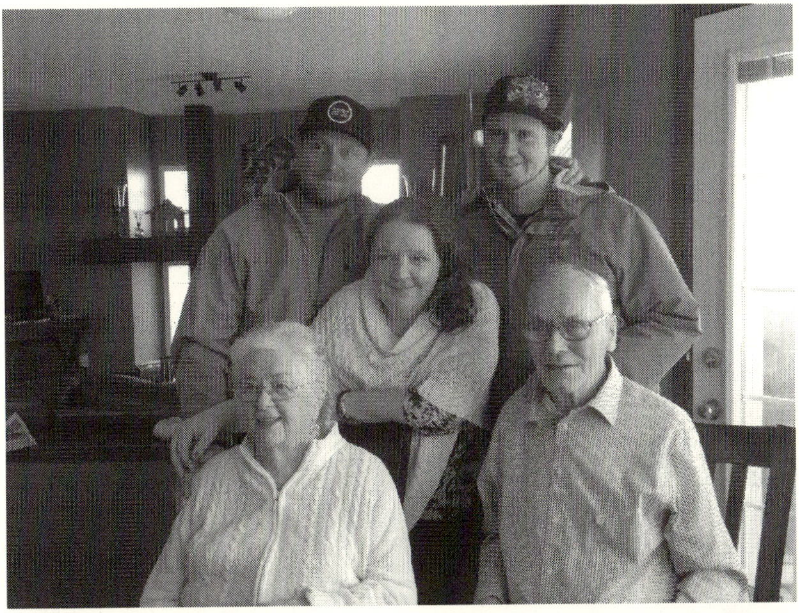

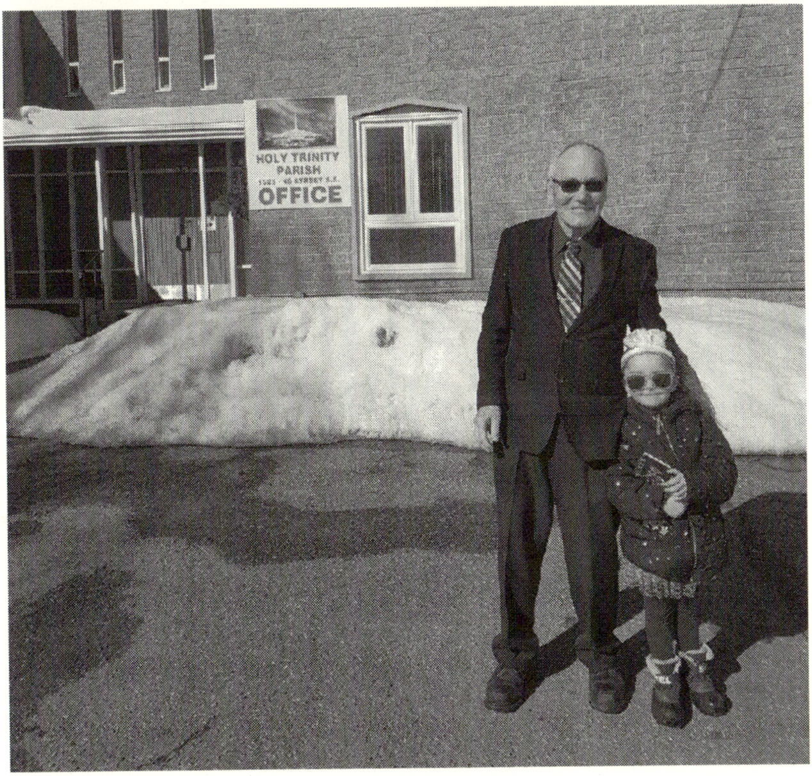
HOLY TRINITY
PARISH
OFFICE

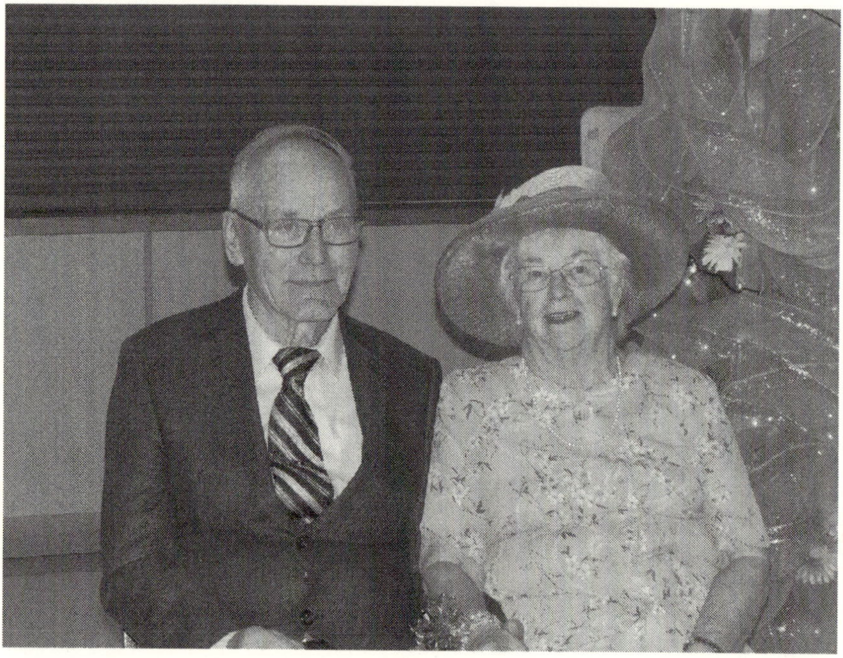

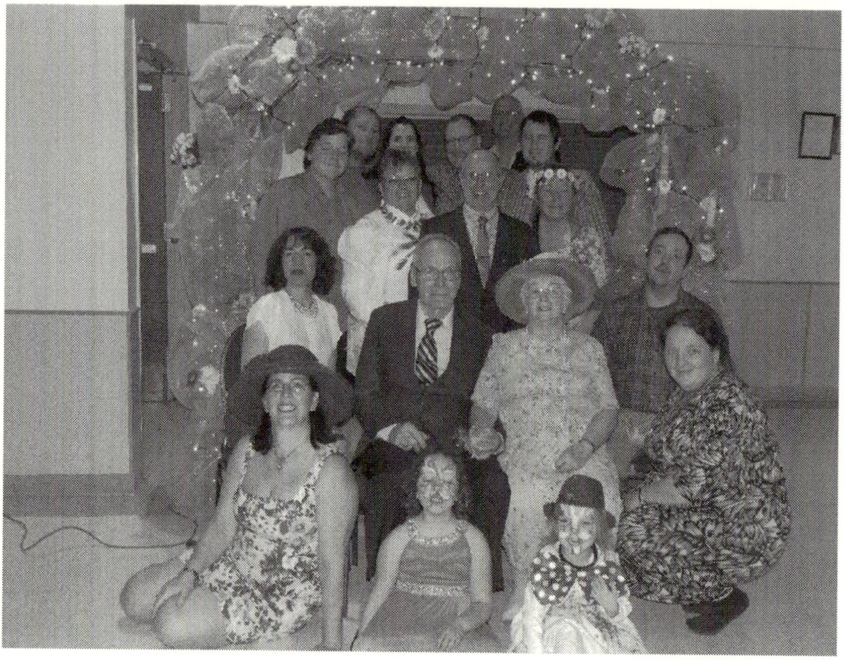

MEMOIRS OF PFN

PAUL FERNAND NEDELEC

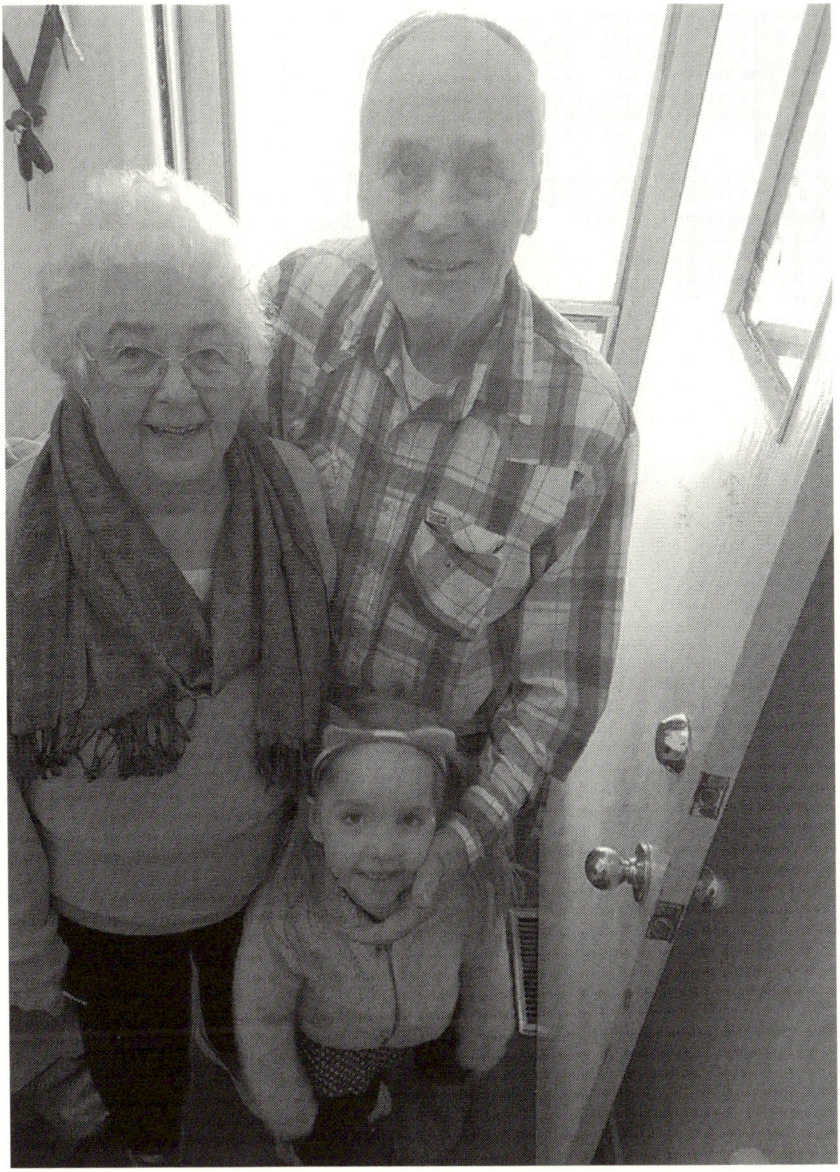

PAUL FERNAND NEDELEC

HE LEFT FOOTPRINTS ON OUR HEARTS

Footprints on My Heart

Some people come into our lives
and leave footprints on our hearts
and we are never ever the same.

Some people come into our lives
and quickly go... Some stay for awhile
and embrace our silent dreams.

They help us become aware
of the delicate winds of hope...
and we discover within every human spirit
there are wings yearning to fly.

They help our hearts to see that
the only stairway to the stars
is woven with dreams...
and we find ourselves
unafraid to reach high.

They celebrate the true essence
of who we are...
and have faith in all
that we may become.

Some people awaken us
to new and deeper realizations...
for we gain insight
from the passing whisper of their wisdom

Throughout our lives we are sent
precious souls...
meant to share our journey
however brief or lasting their stay
they remind us why we are here.

To learn... to teach... to nurture... to love

Some people come into our lives
to cast a steady light
upon our path and guide our every step
their shining belief in us
helps us to believe in ourselves.

Some people come into our
lives to teach us about love...
The love that rests within
ourselves.

Let us reach out to others
and feel the bliss of giving
for love is far richer in action
that it ever is in words.

Some people come into our lives
and they move our souls to sing
and make our spirits dance.

They help us to see that everything
on earth
is part of the incredibility of life...
and that it is always there
for us to take of its joy.

Some people come into our lives
and leave footprints on our hearts
and we are never ever the same.

~by Flavia Weedn~

MARY-ADELE HODGINS' STORY
(Mary-Adele Nedelec – Mrs. Paul F Nedelec)

December 6, 1957, on the Feast of St. Nickolas on a blind date, I met a tall dark and handsome man. Immaculately dressed and a real gentleman; it was love at first sight, almost.

When Paul arrived he wasn't sure which of us, myself or Marion, he was supposed to be on the date with so I boldly claimed that I was his date. In short order I found out that he was a practicing Catholic and that he even had the same missal as me, which I took to be a good sign!

In fact, he had a lot of great qualities that I thought were important. He saved his money, had a bank account and gave me really nice gifts that weren't extravagant. We had similar values and he was lots of fun. All of which mattered to me.

In time I found that he was a hard worker. He taught me to drive and had the patience of Job. What was not to love.

Paul proposed in six weeks. I really liked him, but I wasn't sure by then that I was ready to marry him. I told him he'd have to ask my Father's permission. I thought that was good enough to stall things a little without losing him.

I had come west with my friend Marion and we rented a basement suite. After my first date with Paul, the three of us planned a day of skiing. Paul said he didn't know how to ski, I said I'd teach him what I knew, and before I knew it he was better than me!

After that weekend Paul and I were together almost every day.

We played cards together, we wrote letters home, visited and enjoyed music.

I flew home in March of 1958 and my step mother asked me if there was something serious between Paul and me. I said, "Kind of..."

Paul gave me my engagement ring in April and we decided to get married in December. Paul phoned my father and asked for permission to marry me. My father granted it, but he wasn't sure so he and Kathleen came out in September to meet him. They both liked Paul so December was the date.

Over the years Paul proved that he could fix anything that broke. He always enjoyed making the skating ring and igloo's with glass windows and lighting so the I could see the kids from the house. In fact, he made the whole house by himself.

I touched the outside wall of the house before it was finished and got a shock and he managed to find a nail between 2 wires and fixed it.

We used to go camping, canoeing , play tennis, went biking, hiking, skiing and we even put in huge garden together.

We always had a dog and cats and over the years we had goats that they children took turns milking. Lawrence raised rabbits and sold them. We had 2 ponies, an ex-race horse that liked to come home like the wind. He liked to race Carol's quarter horse and he'd even race semi-truck and trailer units in the ditch alongside the highway. Fortunately for Michelle, he was faster than the truck and beat it across the road into the driveway just in the nick of time. Paul loved to rid with Bernadette, Caroline, Lawrence and Michelle.

Paul taught me to appreciate nature. He has been a most loving spouse. He is the most honest person I have ever known. He's the most hard working. Did I say the most loving person in my life? And, he has never raised his voice that I was aware of. I love him with all my heart. Did I mention that he has the patience of Job?

We have enjoyed many travels which I never expected to be able to do. We went to England, Ireland, France, Australia, Mexico and Hawaii a couple of times, as well as California, Victoria, Kelowna, Trail, Saskatchewan, Ontario, Quebec, New Brunswick, Nova Scotia, PEI, Inuvik in winter and summer, two cruises; one to Alaska and one to Panama. All of which were wonderful!

I really loved skiing, downhill and cross country. The view from the top is spectacular. I wouldn't have gone without him.

Yes, we have had our differences of opinions over the years, but they work themselves out and we still love one another very much in our 60th year of marriage.

Thanks Paul for your company over the years of marriage together. It's been a blast.

Love you and all your participation, caring, sharing and patience. God has been good to us…Very good.

God Bless You!

Hugs and Kisses, Your Loving Wife,

Mary-Adele

AMBER'S STORY

Here are the big questions my Dad taught me:

Am I Happy in what I'm doing ??
How will I be remembered when I'm gone ??
Is what I'm doing going to make Peace and contentment in the world ??

Also he always quoted" Desiderata" to me and it hung on the wall as a reminder.

Do you know that one?? (You are a child of the Universe no less than the trees and the stars you have a right to be here and whether or not it is clear to you -No doubt the Universe is unfolding as it should--) Look it up - It is so Beautiful and so much of my Dad and my childhood with him-that I would include it in his book.

And so we will. And, thanks to Max Ehrmann.

Max Ehrmann

Desiderata

Go placidly amid the noise and haste,
and remember what peace there may be in silence.
As far as possible without surrender
be on good terms with all persons.
Speak your truth quietly and clearly;
and listen to others,
even the dull and the ignorant;
they too have their story.

Avoid loud and aggressive persons,
they are vexations to the spirit.
If you compare yourself with others,
you may become vain and bitter;
for always there will be greater and lesser persons than yourself.
Enjoy your achievements as well as your plans.

Keep interested in your own career, however humble;
it is a real possession in the changing fortunes of time.
Exercise caution in your business affairs;
for the world is full of trickery.
But let this not blind you to what virtue there is;
many persons strive for high ideals;
and everywhere life is full of heroism.

Be yourself.
Especially, do not feign affection.
Neither be cynical about love;

for in the face of all aridity and disenchantment
it is as perennial as the grass.

Take kindly the counsel of the years,
gracefully surrendering the things of youth.
Nurture strength of spirit to shield you in sudden misfortune.
But do not distress yourself with dark imaginings.
Many fears are born of fatigue and loneliness.
Beyond a wholesome discipline,
be gentle with yourself.

You are a child of the universe,
no less than the trees and the stars;
you have a right to be here.
And whether or not it is clear to you,
no doubt the universe is unfolding as it should.

Therefore be at peace with God,
whatever you conceive Him to be,
and whatever your labors and aspirations,
in the noisy confusion of life keep peace with your soul.

With all its sham, drudgery, and broken dreams,
it is still a beautiful world.
Be cheerful.
Strive to be happy.

Max Ehrmann, Desiderata, Copyright 1952.

PAUL TALES

Silently chew on this morsel: Once upon a thyme on my pony-tail trail my Dad Paul would tell us of shocking stories from his way-back-when-the-dinosaurs-roamed prairie farm youth.

His France-French Saskatchewan childhood- would now only be told of in English (unless there were secrets only to be shared with my French fluent mom). Half closing his sky-blue blood-shot eyes, taking in a slow deep breath, deep as the crevasses in the mighty Rocky Mountains they skied upon together, sucking the saliva from the corners of his mouth, my fathers stories would begin.

I adored this handsome dark haired man whom I called "Dad". Being the oldest of the wee brood, I would curl up cozily beside him, as I too hugged my numerous siblings who were stuffed on either side of him on the long couch like teddy bears waiting to be won at the stampede shooting gallery.

Those prairie childhood stories were told to us by my dad during the few special times when he was not at work getting electrocuted on ladders, out in the back field planting thousands upon thousands of Alberta Potatoes, milking the prized four-kid nanny, or tanning the hides of pet rabbits.

Being a hard-working, creative repair/recycle dad he was too busy for telling of tales daily, we had to wait for torrential tempests to get those tales out of him. Once safe inside, all of us noisy young-uns were rarely quiet enough to hear those special stories pass from his usually contemplative lips. But when those medium-rare opportunities occurred we were held in awe by the stark frankness, the wild natural settings, and exotic far-away flavour of Paul's tales.

Poor uncle Andrew loomed large in many tales-he was the "bad guy", the lazy brother, protected unfairly by the all-knowing Blessed Mother, but whipped soundly by the Father on high. Baby Helene personified perfection and all the other brothers-too many to count- were long-gone Charlies. Luckily Andrew was always around to be found at fault for the on-going crises sure to unfold upon that open bald-faced prairie landscape. He was the culprit who missed doing morning chores, who fell out of the barn loft-or worse, pushed our hero Paul, that hard-working angelic little brother out of the home-made tree house into the prickly wild rose bushes. However it happened we cheered on our hero. Poor Uncle Andrew was the lazy good-for-nothing and his little brother Paul was the super farm hero. We knew that to be so because our omni-parental pa's version reflected the wisdom of his ways. Yes my dear dad did shine in all our wee hearts brighter than the setting sun and whiter than the blue moon. Run-away horses, carriage sleds with kicking French Aunties turned upside down in the snow; hidden hunch-backed relatives, scary films featuring the Hunch-back of Notre Dame from Paris and its horse-drawn milk carts, oxen and plows, catching coyote or gopher tales; the oceans of wheat swaying like the waves at sea, it all flowed from the wet lips of my Pa.

Grand-père seemed another villain, with his smoky pipe and red wine bottle, small, aloof, not wanting to play, reading non-stop, always too serious. In contrast Grand-mère, with her loving smile and warmth was always growing the family garden. Paul, their tenth child, sure knew how to play, lucky for us -cards, cribbage, hockey, baseball, throw the bale into the station wagon-he could make anything fun. He built snow forts with slide entrances, rigged out with electric lights and dimmers. My dad even rolled us down the hillside inside a giant wooden barrel-what a blast-talk about dizzy-we couldn't even sit up for hours afterward. Yes, my super-dad rocked. He built snow forts, blanket forts, wooden forts in the fields, sleds, slides, tunnels and giant stars that were bigger than our house and that could be seen for miles upon miles around the sprawling countryside.

He was revered by many and loved by all who knew him well. He was there-showing us how to grow up whenever we showed the least bit of interest in his knowledge.

Paul has his favorite daughter and I knew it was not me. We all knew who she was, especially mom. I did not mind, my favorite mentor was Grand- mère Delphine Selene Blaquiere, Oui, she is still my favorite saint in the whole world. Thus- it only made sense that I was not to be his favored one.

My grandmother Delphine came from Saint Affrique, as a mail order bride. Saint Affrique, (Occitan: Saint Africa), is a commune in the Aveyron department of the Occitan region in Southern France. My grand-mère had worked making Roquefort cheese in the ville de Saint Affrique. She was the only grandmother I knew as my mother's mother had died of breast cancer when my mother was very young. Grandmere Delphine instilled a passion for the French language and culture within me at an early age. In her I saw the seeds of some of my life's desires: to live in a tipi close to a large organic garden with plenty of French liberté, égalité et sororité.

Pa Paul still loves the outdoors. The smell of stepping onto thick and decaying autumn leaves remind me of our family walks and his quiet knowledge of the forest ways. The strong scent of wood being cut still summons my sensory memory of Paul, especially the perfume of pine lumber. Perhaps it is the reason for taking my English name Amber -meaning pine-tree resin. Besides Anne-Marie was easily mangled by those Anglophone rednecks who were calling me Mary-Jane, Betty- Lou or worse yet, country singer, Ann Murray.

The strongest scent that brought my dad close to mind was his fringed smoke-tanned, buckskin jacket. This coat provided a home within a home-a place to hide in the living room closet and heal emotions that needed protecting. I remember some flowery First Nation's beadwork on the top of this treasure but the coat was hanging high and it's long fringe encircled me and provided the shelter and calm within that sweet smelling closet. It was there, surrounded by the loving spirit of my dad, that I would internally recite the sacred Desiderata, a poem which I have always associated with my father:

"You are a child of the universe no less than the trees and the stars; you have a right to be here.
And whether or not it is clear to you, no doubt the universe is unfolding as it should." This poem certainly needed my repeating for I was a doubtful child and in my mind there was NO way this world was unfolding as it should.

Paul's humour sometimes loosened me from my deep thoughts. He was a tease and everyone who knew him had been prey to his teasing. Annie-Bananie-Jamberinie, Nona from Kelowna, the epithets flew out of him like a flushed bevy of quail. All the young ones got affectionate teasing from their Uncle Paul. Occasionally I'd retaliate: Pauly want a cracker? or a harder swipe at his vaunted work ethic: Polly-Wally doodle all day!-that would send him back to his endless outdoor projects like duck hunting, fiddling with electrical wires or in case of a nasty storm, send him to one of the zillion-piece puzzles laid on card tables in his basement man cave.

As a child I wanted to grow up to be Black, dark black! Upon realizing that this was not going to happen I considered using paint to set things right. Since this early childhood desire I've pondered its origins: Was it a hangover from a past life? Was it my Pa's obsession with going to "darkest deepest Africa"? Or was it my grandmother's origins in Saint Affrique (actually the name of a French Catholic Saint)??

His middle name Fernand I also associated him with the tale of "Ferdinand the Bull". Mistaken for furious when stung by a bee under his flowering tree; we knew he was the gentlest bull in the wide open prairie pasture. We trusted him not ever to charge, instead to take his sweet time to smell the beautiful roses. Anyone who observed him in the Bullring would agree.

'Tis difficult to tell where my Super Hero father began and his real larger than life stardom stopped. My own country childhood has become a windy blur blowing from many directions, "witch winds", Chinooks, mystical, of unknown origins and pushing in unanticipated directions-just as the bare-back thoroughbred horse flights have morphed into dirt-road bike races which take a sharp turn downhill towards Jorgensen's thus I find myself thrown down face first to the turf by old Smokey the Stallion.

My hockey coach was dad. It was irrelevant that I could barely skate, of course he wanted his kids playing hockey on the outdoor rink at Conrich!

Was this bone-chilling experience what made me long for Africa, the warm birth land of all humans? Or his yearning to visit a place so far removed from his northern prairie Birth -Farm? The Africa trip still remains a dream for my Dad so I gave him a door-sized African picture book .Plus he must relish the thought of my baby sister Michelle and her partner Brad climbing to the top of Kilamanjaro in Tanzania or dancing with the Masi !

He did go to France with his beautiful wife Mary-Adele, his older sister Yvette and older brother Roger. It was a time for my parents to connect with the ancestors- French ancestors who were country peasants, humble farm folk who toiled on the land from sunup to sunset, who picked the grapes and made the cheese of Southern France, then plowed the fields with oxen teams in the New France Promised Land. Oui, my dad is a soft-spoken prairie farmer who chose the way of a Lover, a Father and one who brings light and warmth to many. He tells his tales in English for his children and French for his dear mère. His years of early rising habits may make him fall asleep before the story's end, but if he takes a snooze we can all rest assured that Paul's tales will continue, because they are alive in us all.

GREAT GRANDPA PAUL NEDELEC…

Where to start… what to say? Paul Nedelec was a Great wonderful and amazing Grandpa to Me (Wynona) and my Brothers Eli and Jan for a long time before he Became a "GREAT" Grandpa to his First Great Grandchild Alexzander in 2003 and then Again to Emma in 2012.

Nope wait let's start again..

Great Grandpa Paul F Nedelec has been the most wonderful and amazing Grandpa to both my Brothers Eli and Jan as well myself for as long as I can remember, Long before he became a Great Grandparent to his first two Great grandchildren Alexzander Nedelec in 2003 and Emma Irie Nedelec Burke in 2012.

Yes better…. Let's continue..

Great Grandpa Paul Has Always Been around as long as I can Remember, Even when we lived far away in Kelowna, the Nedelec Family always seemed not far away. Visits at the lake in Kelowna, Tennis Games and Bike rides! Soo many bike rides!! Summer Bus rides out to visit Grams and Gramps as a child. Grandpa Paul was always there to pick me up from the bus station, usually at some crazy hour like 5 am!! Going to church and holding his big hands, He would always squeeze my hands! Pinching fingers! It has always been the little things, Grandpa always made me feel safe, over 36 years of adventures! Big Fires down by the road roasting hot dogs and marshmallows! Alexzander had his 6th little Fire Man Birthday on the Farm! And, it was far from the first or last awesome party held on the Nedelec Calgary farm. finding the secret hide out above the Garage wallpapered with Calendars! Calendars everywhere even in the outhouse! Camping, Road trips, or just playing cards! I remember the first time I felt I beat grandpa in cribbage (without grandmas help)! I was so proud of myself! I love playing cards with Gramps and Grams! Even a card game Grandpa invented!

Grandpa Paul has taught my siblings, my Children and myself so much over the years like how to tell people "Emma and I came to visit", and not me and Emma! Grammar, manners, Gardening, the list is endless I would not be the person I am today if not for Paul Nedelec. I know I'm still Far from perfect, but he has definitely helped me become a better person.

I remember one time Grandpa Paul was babysitting Alexzander and as we drove away we could see Zander Crying at the window and there next to him was grandpa pretending to cry with him, just when I thought he could not do any better he became a Great Grandpa, and wow! Grandpa Paul is always so good at getting right down with his Great grandchildren and being right in that moment with them. Even at church Grandpa would hold Zanders hand or look at books with him and he would be so good at keeping zander quiet and calm. We really enjoyed that time praying with grams and gramps. I love that they brought God and love into our lives. Now Emma and I go to church from time to time and still sitting next to grandpa and keeping him awake is half the fun ☐ God bless Grandpa Paul And his Wife Grandma Mary-Adele! They have made our lives so much better in so many ways and are so blessed to have them so close to us.

It is home to go see them out at the farm! our happy place, where even the kids want to go! And be outside! I love watching Grandpa Paul play with the kids, whether he is Pulling the cart behind mower with a chair strapped to the back, building a snow fort, a tree house a zip line, just a basic game of x's o's on the old chalk board, building block towers with fire wood downstairs, cards or a story over coffee; there is always something. There is no better place to be than with Great Grandpa Paul, Because you know he will be up to something and ready for a new adventure.

Thanks for always being there for me when I needed you most Grandpa Paul. I know you love me even when I have not always done things the way you or grams wanted, but you have always still supported me and never made me felt ashamed for the mistakes I have made in life. You are one of a kind and I could not ask for better grandparents. You and Grandma brought God into my life, so I know no matter what you will always be there with me and we love you more than words can say. Every day I will pray that you know just how much we appreciate you and everything you have done for us in this life time!

With lots of love and from your First and for a long time Fav Grand Daughter, Wynona …

Wynona Sparrow Crystal Diamond Maria Andrus Nedelec Burke. Also known as Nona xoxox

ALEXZANDER'S STORY

Wynona's Son

Where do I begin? You are amazing in every way possible and I'm so thankful for you to be in my life. For all my life. No one could ask for a better grandpa. You are the king at spades and always will be no matter what anyone says.

I have many memories with you and grandma. Too many that I cannot just choose one. You're the best person in the world to talk to and you're handy with everything you do. Everybody around you agrees when they say they love you and hope you have3 an amazing birthday.

Love you and hope for the best for you.
HAPPY BIRTHDAY

Sincerely,
Zander

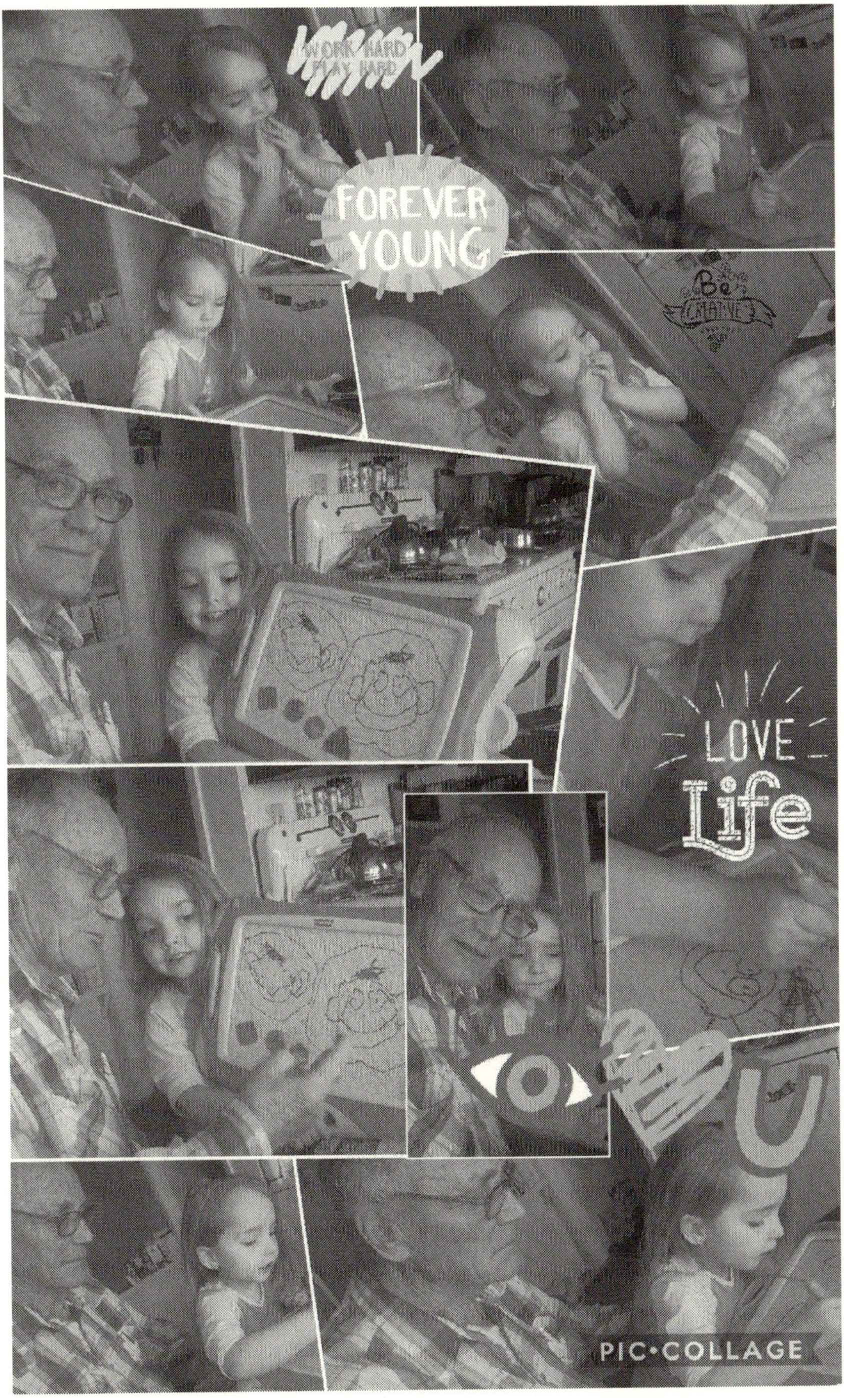
WORK HARD
PLAY HARD
FOREVER
YOUNG
Be
LOVE
Life
PIC•COLLAGE

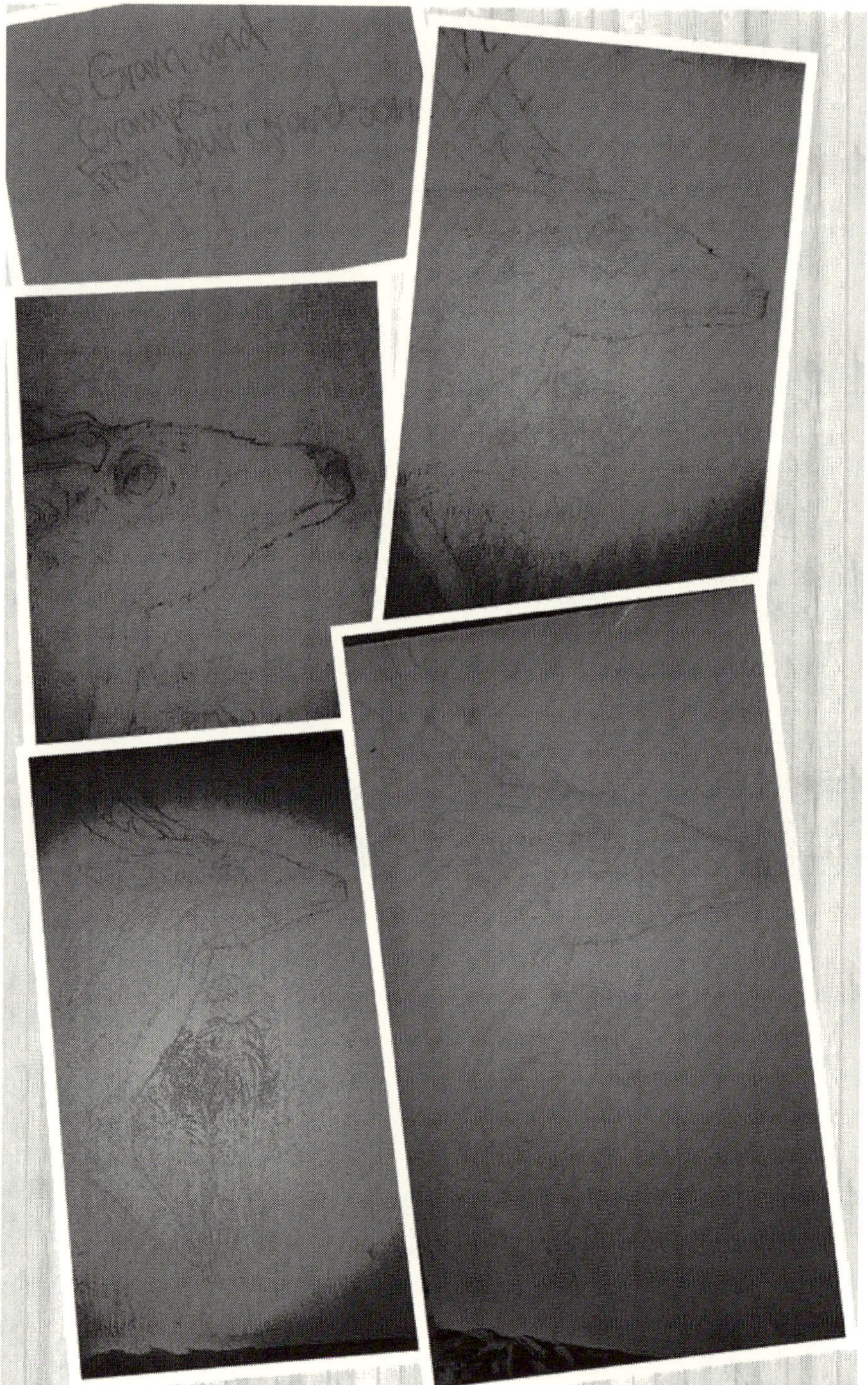
PIC•COLLAGE

JAN'S STORY

My grandpa, Paul Nedelec, was always someone I looked up to and had a huge influence on my life. Any time we got to visit Grandpa Paul on the farm my brother and I were always intrigued by all the things Grandpa was doing. I had a lot of first-time experiences with my grandpa playing sports, doing stuff on the farm camping and having a good time. One time Gramps let me ride along with him on the lawn mower that was one of the best days as a kid for me. Another time he took us ice skating on the pond across the road in the field. I learnt how to skate there with Gramps it was also there where I received a lesson in hip checks by Uncle Lawrence. Gramps had Eli and I were down by the fire until what seemed like the middle of the night burning wood and hay in the bonfire pit. I held a pitchfork of hay over the Flames until my eyes were burning. Gramps always smiled at my attempts to be like him I think he's still smiling today while I keep trying.

I won't forget the times that Grandma and Grandpa would visit us in Kelowna with their camper and stay in front of the house. We would go out and play cards with them in the evenings and go down to the park and play tennis during the day. Grandpa once brought his bow and arrow to Kelowna for a visit, we took it to the park and shot her high in the air. There's a lot of fun memories with Grandma and Grandpa and growing up with them was a blast.

I remember going to Calgary for Christmas almost every year and although we were spoiled with gifts and sweets and food. At Christmas time, my brother and I learn some patience and respect. When it came to Christmas morning, we painfully waited to open presents until after we went to church. We also waited at the dinner table to say a prayer before we ate.

Thanks for all the good times Gramps and happy birthday!.

BERNADETTE'S STORY

If I had to pick two words to describe Dad it would be an "exuberant philomath". To be defined as exuberant someone must be passionate about life, full of energy, excitement, and cheerfulness. And in order to be a philomath, one must love to learn. Throughout his life, in everything he has done, he has taken it on with enthusiasm, determination, and persistence. Whether he was fixing something, building his latest invention, or watching a machine at work, he always seems to know more than anyone else and learn more than anyone else just by looking at something or watching it work. He has an insatiable desire to understand how it works, to know how it was built, and to take on the challenge of fixing it if it is not working. For example last summer, Lawrence's tower fan was not working. Somehow Dad knew how to open it up, which seemed like an impossible task to the rest of us, and of course, he got it working. His work ethic is unmatchable. I believe that he is happier and healthier for the fact that he really has never stopped working, whether it has been paid or unpaid. As an occupational therapist I believe that people are healthier if they are engaged in activities that are meaningful to them. Dad is the archetypical model of this philosophy, and perhaps is the reason that I chose this career path. Mindfulness is all the rage at the moment, but Dad has known how to enjoy the moment for as many as long as I can remember. Have a wonderful birthday and fun reading this collection. C U soon BN.

DUNG'S LETTER

Bernadette's husband

The first time I met Paul was in Montreal. He was visiting Bernadette with Mary-Adele and I was dating Bernadette. I took them out to Bar-B-Barn, a restaurant which specializes in ribs in the western part of Montreal. I picked them up in an old rusty Delta 88 without a muffler. For those of you who were too young to know or do not remember it was a very poor man's Cadillac with a huge engine and two huge creaky doors. It made a lot of noise. I was unemployed, as I had just come back from an extended trip on the Silk Road and driving this ugly, old, beat up car. I still wonder to this day what his first impression of me was?

To me he is the perfect modern day cowboy. Fiercely independent and conservative, but also extremely curious and adaptable. He reminds me of Wilson Bentley, the snowflake man. Wilson Bentley was a self-educated farmer who was the first man to photograph snowflakes in 1885. He went on to photograph thousands of snowflakes, or more accurately snow crystals. He was the first to advance the idea that no two snowflakes are alike. Paul's intelligence cannot be measured by grades, certificates or degrees; you can only experience it by witnessing his desire to learn, to experience and to see new things. His uncanny ability to fix almost anything is remarkable. His patience and his true love of nature are extremely rare in our time where superficiality and low attention span is the norm. The old cliché; "they don't make them like that anymore" truly applies to Paul.

SASCHA'S LETTER

Bernadette and Dung's son

Grandpa, I want to wish you the very best 85th birthday that anyone could ever have. I only wish that I could be there in person to tell you how much I truly love and admire you for the man that you are. You are everything that anyone could ever ask for in a grandfather and more. Thank you for being the wonderful man that you are, and sharing your whole-hearted goodness with me throughout my life. The memories of us spending time together are something that I cherish now and will forever. You are truly a remarkable man.

I love you grandpa!

Happy 85th

Love, Sascha

MIKAELA'S LETTER

Bernadette and Dung's Daughter

When I think of Grandpa, I think of a brilliant mind. I think of someone who uses his brilliance to make other's happy. Like the tray/divider that he made for Grandma's care. She was frustrated because things kept dropping into the space between the seat and the console, so he built something to fill the hole so that she would not be frustrated any more. He also made a picnic table and chairs on a tree stump behind the garage after he cut down a tree. We used this during the pig roast so that everyone could sit down and relax and visit. He built a play house in the trees, just to entertain us kids. My earliest memory if of Grandpa playing hide and seek with Sascha, I and Zander for hours on end! He probably spotted us a couple of times but still let the game continue because the kids were having so much fun. So thank you grandpa for making me and everyone that surrounds you, the happiest we could be. Happy 85th birthday.

Lots of love,
Mighty Mik

WHAT PAUL F NEDELEC MEANS TO ME..

By Caroline Nedelec

The greatest gift I ever received in life came from God & I don't call him Paul F Nedelec I just call him **"my Dad"**

"My Dad" is like no other. All I wanted out of life was LOVE, PEACE, HAPPINESS & a LAMBORGHINI. Well 3 out of four aren't bad I guess. **"My Dad"** was someone I could always relate to and enjoyed being with. **"My Dad"** didn't tell me how to live…he simply lived well and showed me how to do the same. Honesty, trust, having a sense of humour, faith, kindness, intelligence, hard work & delivering more than what you are asked to do were all qualities I learned from **"my Dad"** Some sideline advise to all dads; work hard every day for the special honor to be called **"my Dad"** Not every successful man is a good DAD. But every Good DAD is a Successful MAN!

"My Dad" played while working so if you were lucky enough to catch him removing rocks from the field he would show you how to make rivers rerouting rain water down the driveway. **"My Dad"** would show me how to catch gopher tails and then sell them for money. **"My Dad"** would build snow forts that had picture windows and entire kitchens to play doll house LARGER THAN LIFE! **"My Dad"** would plurk till Midnight & rise the very next morning at the crack of 6 to do it all over again.

"My Dad" also knew the value of excitement and would rig the station wagon up to pull a sled packed with kids in "crazy eights patterns" around the horses pasture driving speeds in excess of 50 MPH. **"My Dad"** would construct handmade death defying contraptions that the neighbourhood Parents were warned about not to play on because they were just too dangerous for their kids. **"My Dad"** would think nothing of letting us hang out the back of a moving vehicle while racing around Saskatchewan dirt roads. **"My Dad"** loved racing the horses & was the first Horse Whisperer I ever met. **"My Dad"** taught me the value of taking risks in life to really go for it!

"My Dad" was not the type to go into great details when it came to personal issues. His Birds & Bees conversation left me even more confused & I couldn't imagine where the stork was supposed to fit in on the whole ordeal.

I remember when I was about 9 years old **"My Dad"** asked me "Do you know what a "Hemorrhoid" is? "NO" Well I just don't think it's something you should be calling your father. End of subject.

"My Dad" was the epitome of a man's man and his hands were so BIG he received the nick name "Paws" from his friends. When we had a rotisserie phone & the holes were too small for his fingers the only way he could dial the phone was with a pen. All of us kids knew better than to be spanked by a man that could reach you with in a ten foot wing span. **"My Dad"** had hands so strong that he could lift you up with one arm and swing you though his legs like a 6 foot tall human swing set.

"My Dad" built his home directly in front of an annual fireworks contest and each year he would help anyone interested to climb aboard his sloped roof to watch the fireworks. In true red neck fashion we would as a family drink beer & enjoy the light show. **"My Dad"** taught me the art of competitive card shark status when it came to board games and cards. My favorite remains to date Spades as it sends shivers down the spine of those weak at heart card novices. It's what we do for fun & some of the greatest sarcasm lines I have ever heard came from these memorable days playing.

Before I met my partner Braden Squirrell **"My Dad"** was my partner in business and we went to Disney World together. **"My Dad"** had no challenge walking four entire parks in three days. (I personally destroyed 4 sets of shoes and had blisters all over my feet.) We also went to Colorado Springs and we both enjoyed our second hot air balloon ride together. The pilot landed so smoothly this time I'm certain we would both temp fate a third time. **"My Dad"** is a great traveler & knows more facts about the world than the 27 full volumes of ENCYCLOPEDIA Britannica he bought our entire family. Before GOOGLE came into fashion **"My Dad"** was the go to guy . He was the man about town that KNEW EVERYTHING & wouldn't mind helping 24/7. Of course this wreaked havoc on my love life because there are very few men in the world that can live up to the talents, skills, and abilities of **"My Dad."**

There are not enough words I can say to describe just how much **"My Dad"** has meant to me and what a powerful influence he continues to have on my life to date. I wish everyone could have been enriched with someone they can call "**"My Dad"** I feel privileged, honoured and grateful for **"My Dad"** Mr. Paul F. Nedelec.

MEMORIES OF POPS

By Braden Squirrell

Well, well, well my name is Braden Squirrell the other half to Caroline Nedelec. I came to know Grandpa; pops on a sunny day. I knew I would like him as he is a trade's person; a "sparky" as we call them. He shook my hand with a firm grip and said hello from that time forward we have come to know one another and I greatly admire the man I have come to know. Caroline told me he likes fire, adventures and things those are dangerous. My kind of guy! Where I am going with this; well as I said the first time I met grandpa I met him as the sun was setting and it was time for a fire. Ok I was in the Park Model and Dad started the fire. I noticed a red glare coming of the side of the park model & ran outside to see a 20 plus feet tower of flames. It was a "doozey" torching most of the tree its way!

Then my first visit out to the old homestead. The place my beautiful baby grew up at. Grandpa said, "Hello son. Good to see you. Have you seen my ZIP-Line? I said No. Out to the back yard he went and said "This is my Zip Line, I haven't been down it in a while so I better test it out for you. I think I could have tested it but no. Down he went; at a raging zip line pace & came to an abrupt stop. Then he said "Yes it's all good!" I was amazed at his get up and go and lack of safety concerns so I went down.

Over time he has become a very special person to me a Dad most would love to have. I hope he understands how special he is, respected and loved. I admire anyone who is living a life he loves, with his special wife and incredible children. Pops you are awesome! Thank you for just being you!

MEMORIES OF MY DAD

By Lawrence Nedelec

The earliest fond memories of my dad were of going on summer holidays to Trail B.C. to visit his brother's and their families or to the homestead near Edam, Saskatchewan and spending time with family and relatives. We also did a couple of big trips to Ontario, Quebec and California.

We developed a keen interest in camping because of Dad's membership in the Knights of Columbus. We owned a trailer of some kind for as long as I recall! We got to learn how to canoe and make great bonfires. (Legendary bonfires) We also had great horseshoe tournaments.

Dad always played sports with me. We would play catch with a softball, go horseback riding with Casey and Starbuck (our horses) and he supported me in my love of hockey with years of early practices, snow removal and warming up frozen feet! Dad taught me how to play cribbage and that I had no future in gambling!

Dad and I had a Saturday ritual of eating downstairs in front of the T.V. watching hockey. In the early days, it was pretty much his Canadiens beating my Maple Leafs, but we eventually both became Flames fans!

Dad was a major contributor in our family having goats, rabbits, horses, cats and dogs. They were the beginning of all of our future interests in four legged friends! Dad built a barn, years after he built the house and garage. The main purpose was to allow me to have my own rabbit business. It was successful from 12 years old until I left home at 18.

Dad and I used to go hunting ducks, geese, partridges and pheasant with his work friends. Dad quit hunting at the same time I could get my license. Coincidence?!?

Many of my best memories with Dad occurred years after I had left home and we became good friends, not just father and son!

Eduglys (my wife) and I loved a place we had travelled to called Huatulco, Mexico. We invited Mom and Dad to go back there with us. It was a great vacation together and is still one of our best holiday memories. We also took a family holiday with almost all the "adult" children and their kids to Tulum, Mexico. This was one of Mom and Dads' last vacations outside of Canada.

In the past several years, the family has been vacationing in Montreal, New Brunswick, house boating in the Schuswap, cottaging and hiking in Waterton or just visiting with relatives at the hunting shack near Edam or with family in Calgary. We are making more memories for the children and grandchildren and great grandchildren! Thanks, Dad!

EDUGLY'S LETTER

Lawrence's Wife

You are one of the most decent person, human beings, I have ever met. Your life's philosophy is one to follow, being caring about family, friends, church, environment and all.

Thank you very much for the wonderful trips, the house boat experience was one of my favourite. Thank you for your support and for being there when we needed you.

We all enjoy spending time with you and grandma, and nobody can beat your wit.

We are so fortunate to have you around. Thank you so much for welcoming me into the family and becomine mine for all these yars.

Love you Grandpa!

God bless you,

Edulglys

EVA'S STORY

Lawrence & Eduglys' Daughter

Grandpa you're the best Grandpa anyone could have!

Thanks for building me a treehouse, zip line, igloo and for going on holiday's with the family and other adventures!

I always enjoy when you and grandma come over for super and especially when we get to stay with you at the time share in Fairmont.

The house boat trip was especially fun. I loved going on the Seadoo with Beau. It was my first time on a Seadoo. I loved when the boat was rocking us to sleep. The floaty behind it was fun too.

I didn't like swimming in the water though. It scared me. I thought the seaweed was going to grab on to my legs and pull me in.

I went on a morning walk with you and we went into the forest to get some sticks. I think it was to build a fire.

Aunty Amber helped us make flower crowns and I really liked them.

Sascha, Mikaela, Emma and I were on the floaties and Emma and I decided to go swimming and Sascha and Mikaela said there really was seaweed way down deep, so we got back up on the floaty.

Thank you for playing games with me like Mexican train!

Thank you for always taking care of Luna, my dog. It means a lot to me that she's always taken care of and I know she's always safe and happy.

I like that you made my dad strong, kind and nice to people. He's always finding stuff for me to do that's good. He always gives me a present even if he can't be there at an event with me. And, he always helps me choose good goals in life. And he's really funny. I know that he gets all of that from you.

Love,

Eva Nedelec

MEMORIES OF MY DAD

By Michelle Nedelec

I remember being younger than 5 and waiting ever so impatiently for Dad to get home. I'd occasionally wake up with him and eat porridge for breakfast that I loved watching him make. It was the only time you'd ever see dad in the kitchen, let alone cooking anything. He'd serve me breakfast and afterwards give me a huge hug and a kiss on the forehead and say, "I love you from here to the Calgary Tower and back."

I'd stare out the window and watch him drive down the oh so incredibly long drive way and watch him begin his commute to the Calgary Tower which we could see clearly out the kitchen window.

When he'd get home I'd be like a puppy waiting for him at the door and before he had time to yell, "I'm home!" which he always did. I'd run off the top of the stairs and jump into his arms.

I may have got too big to jump in his arms but I never got too big to love the honest and sincere hugs that my dad always gives me. Somehow there's never anyone else on the planet in that moment.

My second favourite part of my dad was his death defying self-made playground zones that he built. Whether it was the zip line cable that went from the power pole by the house, across the gravel drive way, over parked cars and hedges for a crash landing into the field, or the 8 foot high slide that dropped at just short of a 90 degree angle with a little J hook at the bottom to fling you through the air. Oh, and you couldn't hold the rail because it was 1 foot pvc and the joints would rip your hands apart so you had to just go for it.

He taught us to be brave that way; get up, get over it, have fun.

He also taught me how to change the oil in my car, which I often did in my 6" stilettoes, which always made Mom giggle.

MEMOIRES OF MY GRANDPA

By Beau Savoie

Grandpa and I have done a lot of things together. Camping, playing cards, building an igloo, mowing the lawn, watching hockey, playing hockey, working on the farm, as well as so much more and there was always one constant; no matter what we were doing, how brilliant or how dull the best part was always spending time with gramps.

I didn't see it at the time but as far back as I can remember he was teaching me; teaching me to be responsible and accountable but teaching me something far more important, he was teaching me how to have fun, how to laugh and enjoy my surroundings. He was teaching me how to learn without my even noticing it, he gave me the freedom to believe I was doing it on my own but I was never alone; he was there watching over me.

When I think of Paul Nedelec, my grandfather, I think of a leader, because leaders are not those who strive to be first but are those who are first to strive, and no one embodies that more than him. As far as I can tell he has never aspired to power, but people are drawn to him, they naturally look up to him and I think that's because we all know no matter what that grandpa will do his best on every day and on every occasion.

I love you grandma and grandpa, you will always be with me!

All my love Beau

(One time when Beau was little, Wynona said something to the effect of, "My Grandpa." Beau said, "That's MY grandpa!" and the fight over the favourite one started all over again with the next generation)

MEMOIRES OF PAUL

By Denis Savoie

There are so many things I remember and love about Paul. The most important of which is that he has always treated me like a son and family. No matter what happened between Michelle and me. He was always kind, considerate and humorous.

The funniest time I remember, is when Paul would fly with Beau up to Inuvik to make sure that he traveled safely. He had it pretty easy because the flight attendants would play with Beau the whole time, carrying him up and down the aisles, playing with him or rocking him to sleep. One time, they came back to him and said, "I think this ones yours!" Beau had a smelly diaper and it was up to Paul to change it! Despite having five children, this was the first time he had to change the pampers. I'm pretty sure he didn't know how. Apparently, there wasn't enough room in the washroom so Paul changed Beau's diaper right there in the isle.

The other thing I remember about Paul was his big mitts. I have never seen such big mitts on a man before. To say it was intimidating would be an understatement. I'm sure he had to give little discipline to anyone ever. They just had to see his hands and politely say, "Yes sir!"

He's been a very gentle bear despite his assets.

MEMORIES OF UNCLE PAUL

By Kathryn x

1993

At 19 years old I was travelling from West to East through Canada and was lucky to stay with Mary-Adele and Paul in Calgary. One evening they suggested a trip to the cinema, but didn't realise until the film started Uncle Paul needed to use his big Nedelec hands to cover my eyes on numerous occasions, why? they had taken me to a film rated R! It was the arty film 'The Piano', and I had to promise not to tell my Dad Charlie about the film choice.

I've just checked now in 2018, it is certification is R for 'severe' sex & nudity. No surprise I haven't risked a cinema trip with them since!

2017

On discussing the strong silent type Nedelec men that married what one might call bolder head strong women, Uncle Paul agreed but added it's also said the men do get the last word.... usual 'sorry' or 'help!'.

Happy Birthday to the cheekiest out of the bunch! have a fabulous birthday party - you deserve it!

Love from your niece, Kathryn

MEMORIES OF UNCLE PAUL

By Nicole Nedelec

No favouritism but, I did like seeing Uncle Paul whenever he came to Saskatchewan. He always had time for us kids and he is the person who taught me how to shoot watermelon seeds! A skill I now pass on to all my friends kids.

Love you Uncle Paul!

Enjoy your special day!

Nikki

MEMORIES OF PAUL

By Patricia Gorman (Wolford)

I don't really have a story about Paul, but more a childhood 'image': I remember the generous spirit of your family dinners. Paul always sat at the head of the table, a true family provider. He always seemed very proud of his family life. I will always remember his way with his springer spaniel dogs and his piercing blue eyes.

Xo Patricia

MEMORIES OF PAUL

By Shaunna Bernardin

I think I first met Paul when I was around 10 years old . I was new to Chestermere that year. I quickly became friends with Michelle and Lawrence we were all on the same bus. Michelle and I hit it off right from the beginning , wasn't long before we were besties.

I would often spend the weekends at the Nedelec house. I remember Paul being very interested in how our day was? He would sit Michelle and I down at the table and ask us things like ... "How was your day girls? Anything special happen today? Did you go outside and get some fresh air today?" Then he would give us some kind of pep talk about remembering to be grateful for what we had and that life was about making good choices. He was never pushy about it, In fact the opposite he always had a remarkable gentle kindness about him .

Michelle and I went downtown to spend the day at work with him. It was a school project but it turned out to be such an awesome day. Paul took his time to explain all the little details of his job to us. He made sure we had all the proper details to fill out our report. Then he hooked us up with a killer private lunch. He even let us go up and down on the elevators a few times he didn't blink an eye. Lol Although we were very young, I remember seeing how much respect everybody in the Building payed Paul that day, everyone we passed would say, "Good morning Paul!" or a give a smile, or a "How ya doing today?" You could tell the entire building liked him. A few years later Paul caught Michelle and I doing something downstairs. It was the craziest thing ever. He just simply asked, "I wonder if you're making good choices girls." He didn't even raise his voice. We straightened up so fast it would make your head spin

I will be forever grateful for your kindness and calmness.

Wishing you a very Happy Birthday, Paul.
I hope you have a great day ☺
Much Love Always,
Shaunna

MEMORIES OF PAUL

I'm sure glad Paul always had a sense of humour and he's so calm. It comes in really handy when he comes to visit us! One time Paul and Mary-Adele came out to the island to visit us with their brand new camper and I convinced them that they should come out to my favourite spot on the island, Pachena Bay. I said, "You'll be fine! The roads good and no there aren't any bears." Ok, I might have stretched the truth a bit. But, it was only because I really wanted them to see it! It's beautiful! So they drove out, down the beat up old dirt logging road with its pot hole, bald heads (the big rocks that pop out of the road) and mountain terrain. When they got there Paul came out to see us and was taken away by how beautiful it was. Mary-Adele, however, was in the trailer putting everything back in the cupboards and taping them down to keep them closed. Meanwhile the poor dog was vibrating when it got out of the trailer.

Eventually we decided to go for a hike down the West Coast Trail. Mary-Adele stayed at camp with our baby, Derek. As we were leaving she says, "Stay Safe!"

I said, "Oh we will, there's no bears here. Sure enough half way into our hike a bear walks across our path. Paul was so calm and just gave me the look of, "Ya sure, no bears here!" We stayed calm and the bear slumbered off. It was a testament to his calm cool reaction. Craig still teases me to this day that it was the day we shook down the Nedelec's.

It's been great knowing you all these years! Getting to meet Bernadette in high schools was fantastic and I'm delighted how well gotten along with her whole family over the years!

All the Best! And, Happy Birthday Paul!

Rosie
Janice Rosenberger

MEMORIES OF PAUL

By Bill Brownridge

Just trying to gather my thoughts. Paul and I have had such a rich and deep friendship, I want to get it right. I have been lucky enough to know Paul for as far back as I can remember. He was a country boy who sometimes road to school on horseback in below zero weather. He was the guy who I shared one of those double desks with in high school - right opposite the Ping Pong table ,(which we raced to get there first at recess or noon break.) He was the friend who helped me on the pathway to art. Paul was visiting on a break from his studies at SAIT in Calgary and showed me the Art College prospectus. He was the friend we shared many family outings and dinners with. He and I enjoyed discussing ideas; politics, religion, world affairs and many of societies difficult questions. Paul and Marie Adele stayed friends with both Bobbie and I through our divorce.

In a lifetime one has many acquaintances but few friends. Paul you have been a rock and a constant source of true friendship.

Happy Birthday PAUL –

Wish I were there!

Bill.

Made in the USA
Middletown, DE
03 May 2018